SCC Library

3 3065 00354 1566

D0558008

VIETNAMESE-AMERICAN
CATHOLICS

BX
1407
.V54
P48
2005

PASTORAL SPIRITUALITY SERIES

VIETNAMESE-AMERICAN CATHOLICS

by

Peter C. Phan

Paulist Press
New York/Mahwah, N.J.

OCM60360324

Santiago Canyon College
Library

Cover art courtesy of Dr. Thu Bui, president of The Vietnamese Institute of Philosophy and Religion. Used by permission. Visit www.vientrietdao.com

The Scripture quotations contained herein are from the New Revised Standard Version: Catholic Edition Copyright © 1989 and 1993, by the Division of Christian Education of the National Council of the Churches of Christ in the United States of America. Used by permission. All rights reserved.

Cover design by Trudi Gershenov
Book design by Lynn Else

Copyright © 2005 by Peter C. Phan

All rights reserved. No part of this book may be reproduced or transmitted in any form or by any means, electronic or mechanical, including photocopying, recording, or by any information storage and retrieval system without permission in writing from the Publisher.

Library of Congress Cataloging-in-Publication Data

Phan, Peter C., 1943–
    Vietnamese-American Catholics / by Peter C. Phan.
        p. cm.—(Pastoral spirituality series)
    Includes bibliographical references.
    ISBN 0-8091-4352-6 (alk. paper)
    1. Vietnamese American Catholics. 2. Church work with immigrants—United States. 3. Church work with immigrants—Catholic Church. I. Title. II. Series.
BX1407.V54P48 2005
282′.73′0899592—dc22

                                                2005012204

Published by Paulist Press
997 Macarthur Boulevard
Mahwah, New Jersey 07430

www.paulistpress.com

Printed and bound in the
United States of America

CONTENTS

Introduction to the Series ix

Preface xi

Chapter 1
Who Are the Vietnamese?
Origins and Identity 1

Chapter 2
How Do the Vietnamese Think, Live, and Worship?
Vietnamese Culture and Religions 20

Chapter 3
How Do the Vietnamese Celebrate?
Vietnamese Feasts and Customs 50

Chapter 4
Who Are Vietnamese Americans?
Living Betwixt and Between in the New Country 64

Chapter 5
Who Are Vietnamese Catholics?
A Brief History of Vietnamese Christianity 84

Chapter 6
Who Are Vietnamese-American Catholics?
Living the Christian Faith in the New World 98

CONTENTS

Chapter 7
What Lies Ahead for Vietnamese-American Catholics?
Pastoral Challenges and Opportunities 127

Chapter 8
How Can I Learn More about Vietnamese Catholics?
Cultural and Religious Resources 137

Ghi nho ngay le tuyen khan trong the cua Nu tu
Maria Benedicta Chua Thanh Than
Nguyen Thi Nhan

Boussu, Bi Quoc
July 16, 2004

INTRODUCTION
TO THE SERIES

The American Catholic Church is an "institutional immigrant" composed of many racial and ethnic groups with diverse religious and cultural traditions. It is also made up of churches that are not "Roman" or "Latin" but derive their religious and cultural heritage from the Orthodox Churches. Earlier groups, mostly from Western European countries, have by and large moved into the mainstream of American society and currently constitute the majority of American Catholics. Recent immigrants and refugees come from other parts of the world, such as Asia, the Caribbean Islands, Eastern Europe, and Latin America. Together with the original native people who were present on the continent before the so-called discovery of the New World, these newcomers have dramatically swelled the ranks of the American Catholic Church. The native peoples and these newer immigrants and refugees—both documented and undocumented—are in many ways a blessing and boon for American society and the American Catholic Church. Recently the U.S. Conference of Catholic Bishops recognized the importance and contributions of these peoples in two statements, *Welcoming the Stranger Among Us: Unity in Diversity* (2000) and *Asian and Pacific Presence: Harmony in Faith* (2001). At the same time, both American society and the Church are facing difficult challenges with regard to these people who are, culturally and religiously, different from their European predecessors and quite diverse among themselves. Part of the difficulty lies in the lack of up-to-date and accurate information on these ethnic groups and their cultural and religious backgrounds.

To help the Catholic Church in the United States carry out its pastoral ministry to all people, Paulist Press is issuing the Pastoral Spirituality Series—books on the cultural and religious heritages of many of these ethnic groups in the Roman as well as Eastern Catholic Churches of America. The ultimate aim of these books is to promote communion in the Church, a communion that recognizes and celebrates the diversity of God's blessings in the ethnic, racial, socio-political, sexual, religious, and cultural richness that all peoples bring to the United States. Such a communion eschews uniformity, and yet seeks to maintain and develop the unity in faith, hope, and love in the service of God's reign.

The publisher, authors, and editors of this series fervently hope that these books will contribute to a better understanding of and appreciation for the unique cultural and religious heritages these communities bring with them to share with the Church in the United States. In the long run, their presence will forge a new type of America and a new model of Church.

Peter C. Phan
Series General Editor

PREFACE

Numbers don't lie. There are now over one million Vietnamese living in the United States. Over 300,000 are Catholic. They form 150 communities or missions, 35 parishes, and 10 quasi-parishes. There are 600 priests, 50 permanent deacons, 700 sisters, and a large number of candidates to the priesthood and religious life. Indeed, it is a well-kept secret that without these Vietnamese priests, religious, and seminarians, many dioceses and religious orders would diminish significantly. Vietnamese-American Catholics, together with their clergy and religious, are equivalent to one of the largest dioceses in the American Catholic Church.

Yet, apart from anecdotes, we know precious little about Vietnamese-American Catholics as well as other Asian Catholic groups. Recently, the U.S. Catholic Bishops took notice of the increasing importance of Asian and Pacific Catholics in their midst. As helpful as their statement *Asian and Pacific Presence: Harmony in Faith* (December 2001) is, it pales beside the statements on black and Hispanic Catholics. More important, it risks becoming a dead letter. There have been no large-scale grassroots gatherings like the Hispanic *encuentros* to galvanize Asian and Pacific Catholics, to listen to their real problems and concerns, to give voice to their dreams and fears, and to plan concrete pastoral strategies and actions. Unless and until these activities are undertaken, with adequate financing and moral support, the statement will only serve as a balm to soothe our pastoral conscience for having taken notice of the presence of Asian and Pacific Catholics in the American Church.

In the meantime, to prepare for these eventual pastoral engagements, we need to know more about these Catholics: their countries of origin, their history, their cultures and religions, their feasts and customs, their Christianity, and the opportunities and challenges these new American Catholics face.

These themes are discussed with regard to Vietnamese-American Catholics in the first seven chapters of this book. Because of limited space, the book can provide little more than essential information, but it is hoped that it will prove helpful to pastoral leaders and those who work for and with Vietnamese Catholics as well as to Vietnamese-American youth who more likely than not do not know their own culture and history well. For further information on Vietnam and Vietnamese Catholics, the final chapter lists some readily available resources.

War pitched Vietnam and the United States against each other and inflicted immense suffering on both countries. However, through Vietnamese refugees, the two peoples have been brought closer together. Through intermarriages and cultural exchanges, through mutual sharing of faith and life, the host and the guest have become one; the eagle, which symbolizes America, and the dragon, which represents Vietnam, have settled down together in the same nest. At the same time, the two Churches have contributed to each other's well-being and growth. It is hoped that this book will help bring about a new type of America and a new Christianity.

This book was completed during the first two months of my service at Georgetown University. I am deeply impressed by the number of Asians in the student body and by the university's commitment to ethnic diversity. I would like this book to be a small token of gratitude to Georgetown University for its efforts on behalf of Asians and Vietnam.

Chapter 1

WHO ARE
THE VIETNAMESE?

ORIGINS AND IDENTITY

The involvement of the United States in the Vietnam War, a twenty-year-long (1955–75) armed struggle between the Democratic Republic of Vietnam (Communist North Vietnam) and the Republic of Vietnam (South Vietnam), and its eventual defeat—the first ever in its history—made Vietnam a household word and even a battle cry for many Americans. The immense financial expenditures and the loss of 58,000 American lives during the war, not counting those who survived as multiple amputees and victims of mental illnesses, had a devastating impact on America's socio-political, economic, and military establishments. The Vietnam Veterans Memorial, in the shape of a polished, black, V-shaped granite wall in Washington, D.C., with the names of the fallen soldiers cut into the 140 different-sized panels, is a poignant reminder of the grim aftermath of the Vietnam War.

The war inflicted even more catastrophic losses on the Vietnamese people. Besides untold suffering and material damage, more than two million civilians and more than one million soldiers were killed and countless numbers were wounded. On April 30, 1975, the forces of Communist North Vietnam captured Saigon, the capital of South

Vietnam, bringing the Vietnam War to an end. In July 1976, the North and the South were officially reunified into a communist state known as the Socialist Republic of Vietnam, with Hanoi as the capital and Saigon changed into Ho Chi Minh City.

An International Presence

Another casualty of the Vietnam War is the immigration of hundreds of thousands of Vietnamese, some known as "boat people," to the West, mostly to the United States. This exile was a traumatic disaster for the Vietnamese refugees, many of whom were pillaged and raped by pirates; others lost their lives to the sea. Tragedy, however, can give birth to blessings. After three decades in the Diaspora, Vietnamese expatriates can look back with pride on their accomplishments in many different fields and recognize with gratitude the opportunities they have been given to make them a truly international people. Vietnamese faces are now seen all over the world and Vietnam as a country is readily recognizable on the map of the globe.

A little incident illustrates well what I mean. Some years ago I was lecturing to a group of Vietnamese of different religious traditions at a Vietnamese Cistercian monastery in Orsonnens, near Fribourg, Switzerland. They had come from the United States, Canada, and Europe for a summer institute on Vietnamese history and culture. While the adults spoke Vietnamese fluently, their children had only a smattering of their mother tongue. During recess, the children played games together, but they could not speak a common language. So they communicated with each other in the languages they knew best. I heard English, French, German, Italian, Portuguese, Spanish, Dutch, Danish, Norwegian, and Swedish spoken simultaneously and without the slightest accent by Vietnamese boys and girls, with a few Vietnamese words thrown into the mix. Happily, it was not a Tower of Babel but a new Pentecost. Though speaking in different languages, the children understood each other well, by a sort of empathy connatural to childhood, and in spite of their new countries of residence and citizenships, they remained distinctly and recognizably Vietnamese. At the same time, thanks to their presence in different countries, their influence extends beyond the narrow confines of their country of origin.

Their Vietnamese identity endures and is even reinforced in the Diaspora thanks to a number of factors. Strong family ties and a number of "Vietnamese towns"—not unlike Chinatowns—with a large concentration of Vietnamese and numerous restaurants and businesses keep the Vietnamese immigrants together. Vietnamese newspapers, radio, television, and Internet websites, readily available everywhere, enable the Vietnamese expatriates to stay in contact with their culture and their ethnic roots. Ease of travel also allows them to go back to their home country for frequent visits and to be in touch with Vietnam's current affairs. New arrivals from Vietnam add to the number of Vietnamese immigrants. Last, and perhaps most important, religious life, especially through churches, pagodas, and temples, offers vibrant communities in which the Vietnamese work together not only to survive in the new countries but also to maintain their ethnic and national identity.

Where Do the Vietnamese Come From?

The Socialist Republic of Vietnam covers 128,400 square miles in Southeast Asia. The country is bordered on the west by Cambodia and Laos, on the north by China, and on the south by the China Sea. The two principal geographical regions, the Red River Delta in the north and the Mekong River Delta in the south, are connected by a long and narrow mountainous strip, with the country curving like a capital *S*. The principal cities are Hanoi (the capital) in the north, Hue (the former imperial city) in the center, and Ho Chi Minh City (formerly Saigon) in the south.

The name *Vietnam* was officially adopted for the country in 1802, but by the middle of the nineteenth century, it was suppressed during French colonization. Vietnam was made part of French Indochina, comprising Vietnam, Cambodia, and Laos. The West came to know Vietnam not by its own official name, but by the names the French gave to its three parts: Cochinchina, a French colony in 1862, for the south; Annam, which became a French protectorate in 1883, for the center; and Tonkin, also a French protectorate in 1883, for the north.

Racially, the Vietnamese represent a mixture of Austro-Indonesian and Mongolian elements. The current population is estimated at 75 million and is growing steadily. It is homogeneous, with 85 percent Vietnamese, but there are fifty-three other ethnic groups, mostly in the north and the central highlands. Before 1975 there were also over one million ethnic Chinese, who were located mostly in Cho Lon, a part of Ho Chi Minh City.

Vietnamese names are listed with the last or family name first, then the middle name, and finally the first or personal name. For example, my name in Vietnamese would be written as Phan (family name) Ðinh (middle name) Cho (first name). Catholics get an extra name, the baptismal name, which is the name of a saint; it is placed before the family name. Normally the middle name indicates gender: Ðinh or Văn for males, and Thi for females. The first name usually carries a meaning, often indicating the character or the destiny the parents wish their child to have (e.g., my first name *Cho* means "to give"). Boys are often given names associated with masculine things such as courage or power, and girls names that convey feminine things such as beauty or nature. The Vietnamese are always addressed or referred to by their first names, which does not suggest familiarity, and not by their family names, preceded by Mr., Mrs., or Ms., or by their professional titles (e.g., Professor Cho). In the United States, the Vietnamese reverse the order of their names to follow American custom, and most of them adopt American names as their first names, followed by their family names (e.g., Peter Phan).

Language and Scripts

The Vietnamese language belongs to the Thai linguistic group and has many Mon-Khmer elements. It is monosyllabic and multitonic; when spoken, it has a singsong cadence. Any word can have in principle at least six tones, each with a different meaning. For example, *ma*, depending on which tone is pronounced, can mean ghost, cheek, but, tomb, horse, or rice seedling. This makes speaking the language difficult for foreigners, especially if they are tone deaf, as mistakes in enunciating the correct tone can lead to disastrous misunderstandings. This happened once to an Italian Salesian priest who, after a long, toneless monologue with a Vietnamese woman, asked her whether she "loved" him, when in fact he meant to inquire whether she had "understood" him.

Until the seventeenth century, the Vietnamese wrote in either the *chu nho* (the Chinese characters or the scholarly script) or the *chu nom* (the demotic or unlearned script), which use a combination of Chinese characters to transcribe and indicate the pronunciation of the Vietnamese words. Needless to say, these two difficult scripts were largely inaccessible to the general populace. To facilitate the learning and writing of Vietnamese, Jesuit missionaries, who came to Vietnam in the early seventeenth century, used the Roman alphabet to transcribe the Vietnamese language and various diacritical marks to indicate its tones. One of the missionaries, Alexandre de Rhodes (1593–1660), though he did not invent the alphabetization, perfected it. Two of his books, a catechism and a dictionary, were published in Rome in 1561 using the new script.

At the beginning of the twentieth century, the French colonial government abolished the use of the Chinese script for state examinations and imposed the Romanized script, both to facilitate popular education and to suppress the political and cultural influence of Vietnamese Confucian scholars. This script, which was originally used only by Catholics, is now called *chu quoc ngu* (the national script) and is in universal use today. No doubt, this script is one of the lasting contributions of the Catholic Church to the Vietnamese culture, even though one may lament the virtual demise of *chu nho* and *chu nom,* since most of the ancient Vietnamese texts were written in either of these two scripts.

Vietnam is commonly described as consisting of three parts: north *(bac)*, center *(trung),* and south *(nam).* This triple division, imposed by French authorities, has geographical as well as political significance. Vietnamese is pronounced in very distinct ways in the three regions. People of the north (from Hanoi to Nghe Tinh) enunciate the five tones distinctly and crisply; those of the center (from Quang Tri to Hue) favor the lower tones and their speech sounds heavy; and those of the south (from Da Nang to Ca Mau) drawl and slur over the tones, reducing the six tones to three. One can easily tell which region a person hails from by his or her pronunciation.

Incidentally, the Vietnamese are often stereotyped according to their geographical and linguistic differences:

northerners are said to be aggressive and formal; those of the center, obstinate and combative; and southerners, pleasure-loving and easygoing. Even the Vietnamese themselves acknowledge that there is a grain of truth in these characterizations, especially when they want to snub people of the other regions!

The Myth of Origin: From the Sea and the Mountain

Like other peoples, the Vietnamese have their own myth of origin. They proudly proclaim themselves to be *con rong chau tien*—offspring of a dragon and a goddess/princess. According to the legend, Lac Long Quan (literally: Dragon Lord of the Lac), the second king of the Hong Bang dynasty and a descendant of the sea god (the dragon), seized Au Co, a mountain princess and the wife of De Lai, a northern (i.e., Chinese) king, and married her (a sanitized version made her the daughter of the Chinese king). She eventually gave birth to a pouch containing a hundred eggs that hatched a hundred boys (one version has fifty boys and fifty girls). So the ancient Vietnamese are said to be the Lac, the earliest recorded name for the Vietnamese people, descendants of the Dragon Lord. Subsequently, fifty went with their mother back to the mountain and fifty followed their father to the sea. Their eldest son was made king of Van Lang, a tiny principality located in the northwest of the Red River Delta near the Chinese border and claimed by the Vietnamese as their first kingdom. Taking the name of Kinh Duong, he inaugurated the first Vietnamese dynasty, the Hung, that comprises eighteen generations of kings.

This myth of a common parentage, which comes in various versions and is devoutly memorized by successive generations of Vietnamese children, serves to strengthen the unity of the people and to urge solidarity among them. It also represents the geography of Vietnam, which is flanked on the one side by a mountain range, the home of its mother, the princess/goddess, and on the other by the sea, the dwelling-place of its father, the dragon. In addition, it also intimates the unification of the two fundamental elements of the Vietnamese culture, the aquatic or sea-oriented line of the south and the continental or mountainous line of the north, the former symbolized in Vietnamese mythology by the Water Spirit and the latter by the Mountain Spirit. Lastly, the myth serves a useful political function: it demonstrates the ability of the Vietnamese (the Lac Long Quan element) to appropriate the civilization of the Chinese (the Au Co element). Hence, the Vietnamese have no need of the "civilizing" mission of the conquering Chinese.

The origins of the Hung dynasty are of course lost in the mythic past, but its beginnings are dated by archeologists to the Phung Nguyen culture of the late third millennium BC, belonging to the advanced Neolithic or early Bronze Age. However, archeological finds such as blades for daggers, halberds, swords, points for javelins and lances, arrowheads, crossbow triggers, hoes, plowshares, scythes, sickles, and drums, all made of bronze, reveal that by the seventh century BC, the early Vietnamese had formed a stable society (the Lac society), inhabiting a single geographical area (the plains of North Vietnam), and had achieved a civilization called Dong-Son, after a village near Thanh Hoa, where evidence of the bronze industry was first discovered. These remains suggest that these people came from both the mountain and the sea, lived in a feudal society, and made their living by means of agriculture (mainly rice-growing) and fishing.

Ironically, the first figure documented by reliable sources in Vietnamese history is not a Vietnamese but a

Chinese invader. In 222 BC, in China the state of Ch'in conquered the state of Ch'u, and in the following year, Ch'in Shih Huang Ti (literally, the First Emperor of Ch'in, who, incidentally, ordered the Great Wall built) sent half a million soldiers to invade the Yüeh (or Viet) lands located in the delta lying south of the Yangtze River. Subsequently, a man by the name of Thuc Phan dethroned the last of the Hung kings of the Lac people, took the title of King An Duong, and founded the kingdom of Au Lac. Eventually, his kingdom fell to another Chinese by the name of Chao T'o (Vietnamese: Trieu Da). Chao T'o, who had adopted the customs of the Viets, invaded Au Lac in 207 BC, dethroned An Duong, and ruled over the new kingdom called Nam Viet (Chinese: Nan Yüeh) for over seventy years. He died in 136 BC, allegedly at the ripe old age of 121 years. For the first time in their history, the Vietnamese people were part of a kingdom, founded by Chao T'o, that encompassed all of south China.

History of Oppression and Struggle for Liberation

For our purposes it is not necessary to narrate in detail the subsequent history of Vietnam with all its twists and turns. Rather, to grasp the Vietnamese national character and Vietnamese culture, we take a bird's-eye view of Vietnam's history, which is one of centuries-long oppression and repeated struggles for liberation. A famous Vietnamese songwriter, Trinh Cong Son, summarizes the history of Vietnam in a single verse: "A thousand years of Chinese domination, a hundred years of French rule, twenty years of daily war [between North and South]."

This constant battling for freedom and national sovereignty against foreign domination has instilled in the

Vietnamese a deep love for their country and an unabashed pride in their national heroes. Furthermore, centuries of fighting against more powerful enemies have molded the Vietnamese into long-suffering, resilient, and resourceful survival artists. Interestingly, the totem animal of the Vietnamese (as well as the Chinese) is the dragon, which is a symbol of power, imperial sovereignty, and immortality, and their symbolic tree is the bamboo, which bends but never breaks and therefore represents strength, resiliency, and permanence.

One Thousand Years of Chinese Domination (111 BC–AD 939)

Vietnam has had a longstanding love-hate relationship with China, its powerful and vast neighbor to the north. In 111 BC, the Han dynasty, which had succeeded the Ch'in in 207 BC, conquered Nam Viet as part of its imperialist policy of territorial aggrandizement. It organized the newly acquired land into seven prefectures, three of which—Giao Chi, Cuu Chan, and Nhat Nam—constitute part of North Vietnam today. Chinese domination over Vietnam lasted 1,050 years, interrupted by periodic insurrections, until Vietnam gained independence in 939. During the next nine hundred years of Vietnam's independence and growth, from the liberation from the Chinese rule in 939 to the French occupation in 1862, China, especially during the Yüan (Mongolian) (1260–1368) and the Ch'ing (Manchu) dynasties (1644–1912), attempted several times to regain domination over Vietnam, but their efforts were defeated. It was only under the Ming dynasty that China was able to reconquer Vietnam in 1407, and their extremely harsh rule was not broken until 1428.

To understand the Vietnamese national character and culture, it is essential to grasp the ambivalent relationship between Vietnam and China. The latter's policy has traditionally been either to dominate the former as its vassal or, failing that, to keep it weak and divided. Needless to say, China's ten-century-long domination over Vietnam and its policy of Sinization (imposition of all things Chinese), especially during the Ming occupation, inspired nothing but suspicion and hatred in the Vietnamese toward their colonizers. Even today, the Vietnamese continue to look upon the Chinese with distrust and antipathy, and in some quarters *Chinese (ba tau)* is a term of abuse. At the same time, Vietnam's struggle for freedom against China has produced heroes, both women and men, whose memories are marked with yearly national celebrations and of whom we will speak below.

Historians rightly marvel at the fact that the Vietnamese people, unlike their neighbors, were able to resist the Chinese thousand-year-long policy of Sinization and retain their distinctive language, culture, and national identity. There are many reasons for this astounding feat. Geographically, Vietnam was on the periphery, far from China's cultural centers. On its southern border, Vietnam was contiguous to and had frequent contact with the kingdoms of the Chams and the Khmers and could look upon their Indianized cultures as an alternative to the Chinese way of life. The Vietnamese language, which is different from Chinese, served as an extremely potent barrier against the infiltration of Chinese thought and as a tenacious repository of the pre-Chinese civilization. Lastly, the Vietnamese peasants in their villages, who at any time constituted 80 percent of the population, were largely untouched by the Chinese high-brow culture that the Chinese-educated upper class of Vietnamese society tried to promote. They continued to cling stubbornly to their local, pre-Chinese customs and religious practices.

On the other hand, ironically, where the Chinese failed to achieve, the Vietnamese kings, especially from the time of national independence in 939, succeeded admirably. To unify and strengthen their young kingdom, they looked to China for models of socio-political organization, law, administration, education, and even religion. As we will see in the following chapter, thanks to this voluntary Sinization, enthusiastically adopted by the upper class, in spite of a deep-rooted hatred of China, Chinese influence on Vietnam is deep and extensive. It covers all aspects of society, administration, education, culture, and religion, so that Vietnam can be said to be, to use the title of Joseph Buttinger's book on Vietnam, "the Smaller Dragon," a replica of the "Great Dragon" that is China.

National Heroines and Heroes

Before moving on to the next phase of Vietnamese subjugation by foreign power, let's take a brief look at the Vietnamese heroines and heroes who have contributed to the independence of Vietnam from China and whose names and exploits are invoked with pride in any conversation about Vietnam's past.

The first three persons leading insurrections against China were women, suggesting that ancient Vietnam was a matriarchal society. During the Han occupation, one of the prefects of Giao Chi by the name of Su Ting was greedy and inept. In AD 40, Trung Trac, wife of Thi Sach, and her younger sister Trung Nhi led the insurrection and expelled the Chinese. Trung Trac was proclaimed queen of the newly independent country. A year later, the Han sent one of its best generals, Ma Yüan (Vietnamese: Ma Vien), to reconquer the land. After a few initial victories, the Trung sisters were defeated and killed in 43. According to another tradition, instead of surrendering, they committed suicide by jumping into the Hat River. The Trung sisters, popularly known as Hai Ba Trung (The Two Ladies Trung), are the most revered heroines of Vietnam. Two pagodas, one in Hanoi and the other in Son Tay, were erected in their honor. The anniversary of their deaths (the sixth day of the second month of the lunar year) is celebrated as Vietnamese Women's Day.

Another woman who led a rebellion in AD 248 against the Chinese under the Wu dynasty was Trieu Au (Lady Trieu). To her brother who advised her against organizing an insurrection, she is supposed to have replied: "I want to ride a strong wind, crush with my feet the engulfing wave, kill the whale of the Eastern Sea, purge the land of foreign enemies to save the drowning people. I do not want to follow the example of those who bow their heads and bend their backs to become concubines of the Chinese." After several months of fighting, she was defeated and killed at the age of twenty-three. Depicted in Vietnamese folklore as a fearless leader, going into battle astride an elephant, her yard-long breasts thrown over her shoulders, Trieu Au epitomizes the Vietnamese woman's courage and patriotism.

The military hero credited with securing the independence of Vietnam from China in 939 is Ngo Quyen (898–944). Under the Southern Han dynasty the Chinese attempted to annex Vietnam. Liu Hung-ts'ao, the Han ruler's son, was put in charge of the expedition. He moved his army up the Bach Dang River into the heart of Vietnam. Anticipating his enemy's movement, Ngo Quyen had his men plant a barrier of sharp iron-tipped poles that reached just below the water level at high tide. When the Chinese arrived at the mouth of the river, Quyen sent out a small fleet of light boats at high tide to entice the enemy to pursue them. As the tide fell, the heavy Chinese warboats were all caught on the poles and were fiercely attacked. Half of the Chinese were drowned, including Liu Hung-ts'ao. This famous victory is known in Vietnam as the battle of Bach

Dang. Incidentally, the same tactic would be used later by another Vietnamese national hero, Tran Hung Dao, in 1288 against the formidable Mongolians, who suffered defeat for the first time at the hands of the Vietnamese.

Two other national heroes are Le Loi, who in 1427 liberated Vietnam from the rule of the Ming dynasty and founded the Later Le dynasty, proclaiming himself king with the name of Le Thai To, and Nguyen Hue, who defeated the Manchu invasion in 1788 and became king, taking the name of Quang Trung and founding the Tay Son dynasty.

Trung Trac, Trung Nhi, Trieu Au, Ngo Quyen, Tran Hung Dao, Le Loi, and Nguyen Hue, and many others are the men and women proudly proclaimed by the Vietnamese as their national heroes and heroines.

One Hundred Years of French Rule (1862–1954)

After Vietnam's independence from China in 939, a series of eleven dynasties succeeded one another as rulers of the country: the Ngo (939–967), the Đinh (968–980), the Early Le (980–1009), the Ly (1010–1225), the Early Tran (1225–1400), the Ho (1400–1407), the Later Tran (1407–13), the Later Le (1428–1788), the Mac (1527–92), the Tay Son (1788–1802), and the Nguyen (1802–1945). Of these, the Ly, the Early Tran, and the Later Le dynasties, which together occupied the throne for more than seven hundred years, contributed the most to the development of the country in all aspects of life. Part of this development consisted in the territorial expansion toward the south (Vietnamese: *Nam Tien,* literally, March to the South)—not unlike the American March to the West—which led to the conquering of the kingdoms of the Chams and the Khmers. Thus, sadly, Vietnam, which had endured a thousand years of Chinese domination, in turn developed imperialistic ambitions of its own. It conquered and erased from history the

Indianized kingdom of Champa, and by the end of the eighteenth century, it also took control of the Mekong River Delta, part of Cambodia.

From the Christian point of view, the two dynasties that are most significant are the Later Le, especially during the last two centuries of its existence, and, more important, the final dynasty, the Nguyen. As we explain at greater length in chapter 5, Catholic Christianity was introduced into Vietnam in the early sixteenth century, but Christian mission really took off only from the third decade of the seventeenth century. By the nineteenth century, the Christian church in Vietnam had developed into a well-organized institution of about thirty thousand souls, with a steady influx of foreign missionaries into the country.

One of the curses that attended the coming of Christianity in Asia in general and in Vietnam in particular was its involvement in Western military and mercantile imperialism. First, Portugal, then Holland, France, and England (each of the last three countries founded an East India Company to serve its commercial interests) looked upon Asia as the place where they could expand their political influence and from whose inexhaustible resources they could enrich themselves. On their part, the Vietnamese rulers sought to take advantage of foreign trade and military assistance to vanquish their political rivals in their internecine wars.

In his war against the Tay Son dynasty, Nguyen Anh, who founded the last Vietnamese dynasty in 1802 and who took the name of Gia Long, was greatly assisted by French Bishop Pierre Pigneau de Béhaine (1741–99). When Gia Long's successors—Minh Mang (1820–40), Thieu Tri (1841–47), and Tu Duc (1848–83)—jailed and killed French missionaries (of which we speak at length in chapter 5), France used this persecution as a pretext to invade Vietnam in order to gain a foothold in the commerce with Asia. France's conquest of Vietnam began with an attack on Da Nang in 1858. In 1862 the French government forced Tu Duc to sign a treaty making the southern part of Vietnam (Saigon and the three adjoining provinces) into a French colony, now named Cochinchina, and in 1883 both Central and North Vietnam were made French protectorates, with the names of Annam and Tonkin, respectively. Tu Duc was the last emperor of an independent Vietnam; his nine successors in the Nguyen dynasty were little more than puppets of the French colonial government. Thus began Vietnam's second longest domination by a foreign power.

As with the Chinese domination, Vietnam's struggle against French colonization produced a number of national heroes. The best known among them are Ho Chi Minh (popularly known as Uncle Ho) and Ngo Dinh Diem. The French army was dealt a decisive defeat at the famed battle of Dien Bien Phu by the Vietnamese army under the command of General Vo Nguyen Giap and surrendered on May 8, 1954. As a result, an accord was signed in Geneva on July 20, 1954, stipulating that Vietnam would be temporarily split into two areas, with a Demilitarized Zone along the seventeenth parallel. The North would be governed by the Democratic Republic of Vietnam (under the leadership of Ho Chi Minh) and the South by the French Union until 1956, when there would be general elections to decide whether Vietnam should be reunited in one country.

Twenty-Year Warfare between North and South (1954–75)

The projected plebiscite with the reunification of the country on the ballot never took place. Nine years before the Geneva Conference, on September 2, 1945, Ho Chi Minh (1890–1969) had proclaimed the independence of Vietnam under the name of the Democratic Republic of Vietnam (DRV). His declaration opened with words taken from the American Declaration of Independence: "All men are created equal. They are endowed by their Creator with certain inalienable rights; among these are life, liberty, and the pursuit of happiness." Subsequently, assisted by Communist China and the Soviet Union and inspired by Marxist ideology, Ho Chi Minh attempted to unify the whole country under communist rule. The Geneva Accords, which did not stipulate an immediate unification of Vietnam under communist rule, were a great disappointment to DRV leaders. Hence, they pressed vigorously for national elections, which had been mandated by the Geneva Accords and which they anticipated winning easily.

Meanwhile, in South Vietnam, Ngo Ðinh Diem (1901–63), a Catholic and a strong anti-Communist, was asked by Emperor Bao Dai (the last king of the Nguyen dynasty) to head the government. After his victory over Emperor Bao Dai in a referendum, Diem proclaimed the South to be the Republic of Vietnam (RVN), with himself as president, on October 26, 1955. The United States considered Diem the best alternative to Ho Chi Minh and communist rule and supported Diem in his refusal to hold the elections stipulated by the Geneva Accords. However, Diem's rule soon grew unpopular, and disaffection became widespread. On November 1, 1963, with the approval of Washington, a coup was launched. Diem and his controversial brother, Ngo Ðinh Nhu, were arrested and killed the following day.

Following Diem's death, the war between North Vietnam and South Vietnam escalated dramatically. Already in December 1960 the North had created the National Liberation Front and its military branch, popularly known as Viet Cong, to take over the South. The war dragged on for twenty years, with the United States getting more involved militarily (by the end of 1968, the number of Americans serving in Vietnam had grown to 525,000). Beginning in 1968, Washington began looking for a way out of the Vietnam quagmire. On January 27, 1973, an agreement was signed in Paris to end direct U.S. military involvement in the conflict. The Paris Peace Accords did not, however, end the war itself. On the contrary, fighting grew fiercer and was not ended until April 30, 1975, when the communist forces of the North captured Saigon and the South capitulated. In 1976, the two parts of Vietnam were officially reunited in a communist whole as the Socialist Republic of Vietnam.

A Country under Reconstruction

The decade immediately following the unification of Vietnam was an extremely difficult period for the Vietnamese people. Political purge through reeducation camps, forced relocation of city people to "new economic zones," economic embargo by the United States, invasion of Cambodia and border war with China in 1979, rapid population increase, farm collectivization, currency reform, natural disasters—all this brought about widespread famine and misery. Only in 1986 did living conditions begin to improve when the communist leadership instituted a more open economic policy called *doi moi* (renovation), which permitted limited forms of free market economy.

Politically, Vietnam and the United States, under President Carter, explored the possibility of establishing diplomatic relations in 1977, but talks collapsed when Vietnam demanded billions of dollars in war reparations. Obstacles were also posed by the issue of American military personnel missing in action (MIA). In July 1985, Vietnam permitted U.S. inspection teams to visit probable MIA burial sites and provided Americans access to war records, archives, and cemeteries. Furthermore, the United States demanded that Vietnam withdraw its troops from Cambodia, which it had occupied in 1979 (Vietnam finally did so in 1989). As a result of these moves, under President Clinton, the American trade embargo was lifted in February 1994, allowing U.S. trade and investment. In January 1995, U.S. and Vietnamese officials signed an agreement exchanging liaison officers, and in July of the same year, President Clinton established full diplomatic ties with the Socialist Republic of Vietnam. Symbolically, with the raising of the American flag over the American embassy in Hanoi on August 6, 1995, the two countries were formally reconciled, and a new chapter in the history of American-Vietnamese relations was inaugurated.

Chapter 2

HOW DO THE VIETNAMESE THINK, LIVE, AND WORSHIP?

VIETNAMESE CULTURE AND RELIGIONS

A people's genius and ethos, often conditioned by their geography and history, are expressed in their cultural and religious traditions. Hence, to understand the Vietnamese one needs to know not only their land and history, which we looked at in the previous chapter, but also the pattern in which they think and organize their daily life as well as the ways in which they relate to the transcendent. In other words, some familiarity with the Vietnamese culture and religions is required.

Culture and Religion

Even though the conventional distinction between culture and religion is adopted here, it must be remembered that the borders between culture and religion, especially in Asia, are extremely porous and by no means clearly identifiable. In Asia, religion does not always have an institutional organization distinct or even separate from culture and society.

Indeed, if religion is understood as a social and bounded organization with a creed, cult, code, and community of its own, as is often the case today in academic studies of religion, many Asian religious traditions such as Confucianism and Taoism would not qualify as religion.

In Asia, religion is generally understood as a way of life. The Vietnamese word for religion is *đạo,* meaning path, road, or way. Of course, beliefs (creed), worship and prayer (cult), ethical norms (code), and common, especially monastic, life with an authoritative hierarchy (community) are by no means absent in Asian religions. But they form significant parts of Asian religions only insofar as they promote a way of life leading to a full flourishing of humanity (Confucianism), union with the cosmos (Taoism), liberation from suffering (Buddhism), or a total submission to God's will (Islam). As ways of life, these religions are deeply intertwined with and inseparable from Asian cultures. In a sense, culture is the outward manifestation of religion, and religion is the depth dimension of culture. The one cannot be understood apart from the other. Hence, it is necessary to consider Vietnamese culture and Vietnamese religions together.

Culture as an Integrative Whole

To obtain a practical understanding of Vietnamese culture, it is helpful to adopt the anthropologist Louis Luzbetak's description of culture as: "(1) a plan (2) consisting of a set of *norms, standards,* and associated *notions* and *beliefs* (3) for *coping* with the various demands of life, (4) shared by *a social group,* (5) *learned* by the individual from the society, and (6) organized into a *dynamic* (7) *system* of control."[1]

---

1. Louis Luzbetak, *The Church and Cultures: New Perspectives in Missiological Anthropology* (Maryknoll, NY: Orbis, 1988), 156.

In terms of its constitutive elements, again according to Luzbetak, culture can be said to be composed of three levels: the first, or surface, level is made up of the who, what, when, where, how, and what kind (culture as material, or the signs or symbols of culture). The second, or intermediate, level is the meaning or message of these signs and symbols (culture as ideational), which is constituted by the linkages among the signs and symbols and is revealed in the immediate whys. The third, or ultimate, level is the deeper meaning, the ultimate reasons, the ethos or mentality of a people deriving from the underlying premises and assumptions of their thought processes, the values and interests of their basic attitudes, the goals and ideals of their fundamental motivating forces. This level of meaning, highly resistant to a clear articulation, is the profoundest part of culture as ideational and is hidden in a people's worldview, myths, rituals, philosophy, and religion.

Finally, each culture has codes or rules according to which the intermediate and ultimate meanings are expressed. Like the grammar of a language, codes are the basic rules according to which cultural signs and symbols function and which must be observed to express their meanings correctly. As Robert Schreiter explains, they "encompass the rules of action of a culture, of what is done and what is not to be done. In so doing, they not only define the range of activity of the signs, but can also tell us something of basic messages."[2] These codes govern culture as performance.

This view of culture sees it as an integrated and integrative whole, a distinct way of life of a particular group, with its own material things (culture as material), meanings

---

2. Robert Schreiter, *Constructing Local Theologies* (Maryknoll, NY: Orbis, 1985), 67.

(culture as ideational), activities (culture as performance), and behavioral norms (the cultural code), into which the members are socialized and which rewards those who conform to and punishes those who deviate from them. In this and the following chapters I describe the Vietnamese culture understood in this sense, that is, its material things together with their intermediate as well as ultimate meanings and its feasts and customs.[3] In chapter 4 I draw attention to the struggles and challenges facing Vietnamese Americans as they attempt to adapt to the American culture, which is not a sharply demarcated, self-contained, homogeneous whole but is a historically evolving, fragmented, conflicted, ever-shifting, and porous social reality.

---

3. In this book I am using "Vietnamese culture" to refer to that which is common to the Viet ethnic group (also known as the Kinh) who, as has been pointed out in chapter 1, make up over 85 percent of the current population of Vietnam. Beside the Viets, there are fifty-three other ethnic groups, each with a distinct culture. Geographically, Vietnamese culture as a whole can be divided in six regions: (1) Northwest (mainly Thai), (2) Northeast (mainly Tay and Nung), and (3) Northeast (mainly Viet) in the north; (4) the Coastal Plain (mainly Champ and Viet) and (5) the Highlands (mainly Mon-Khmer and Malay) in the center; and (6) the south, mainly Viet, comprising the so-called Six Provinces (Bien Hoa, Gia Dinh, and Dinh Tuong in the southeast, Vinh Long, An Giang, and Ha Tien in the southwest). Historically, Vietnamese culture can be divided into six periods: (1) The prehistoric, Paleolithic Age (about 10,000 BC). (2) The formative, Neolithic and Bronze Age (about 1000–179 BC). This period comprises the Dong Son, Sa Huynh, and Dong Nai cultures. (3) The constitutive period (the first millennium AD). During this period, Vietnam was under the influence of Chinese culture from the north, and in contact with the Champ culture in the center, and with the Oc Eo culture in the south. (4) The classical or independent period, under the various Vietnamese dynasties (938–1858), during which Vietnamese culture was definitively shaped. (5) The period under French colonization (1859–1954), during which Vietnamese culture underwent drastic changes due to the influence of Western ideas and technology. (6) The contemporary period (1955–), during which Vietnam had extensive contacts with the United States and other countries.

Vietnamese Culture

Limited space restricts what can be said about Vietnamese culture; only the barest essentials are presented here regarding the norms, standards, notions, and beliefs with which the Vietnamese people as a social group cope with life. Furthermore, "culture" is an abstraction. In our dealings with the Vietnamese, we encounter not Vietnamese culture but Vietnamese women, men, and children. These individuals are not specimens of Vietnamese culture, and therefore should not be stereotyped according to a preconceived notion of Vietnamese culture. Whatever understanding of Vietnamese culture that can be gleaned from this book should only serve as a rough-and-ready guide to grasp why the Vietnamese people think, live, and worship in a particular, and at first sight, at least to outsiders, rather strange, way.

Heaven, Earth, and Humanity in Harmony

How do the Vietnamese see the world? It is difficult if not impossible to describe precisely the Vietnamese worldview. Part of the problem lies in the fact that Vietnam does not possess a literary and philosophical canon of its own comparable to China's Five Classics and Four Books, even though these works were adopted by Vietnam as the basis for individual learning as well as preparation for government service from the thirteenth to the early twentieth centuries. The traditional Vietnamese worldview is expressed not in philosophical works but primarily in folk oral literature consisting of myths and legends, proverbs and folksongs; in works of literature, especially poetry; and in ethical and religious practices.

Among the many concepts and values that are central to the Vietnamese culture, harmony obtains pride of place. The Theological Advisory Commission of the Federation of

Asian Bishops' Conferences, in its 1995 lengthy study enti-tled *Asian Christian Perspectives on Harmony,* says that har-mony constitutes "the intellectual and affective, religious and artistic, personal and societal soul of both persons and institutions in Asia."[4]

The Vietnamese word for harmony is *hoa hop* (literally: joining together peacefully or peaceful union). Harmony is not something that just happens; rather, it is something we intentionally and deliberately work to bring about, often with great effort and sacrifice. Furthermore, harmony is the opposite of unanimity. The constitutive elements of unanim-ity are all identical, or at least similar, and differences are eliminated on principle. Harmony, on the other hand, is something created out of many, diverse, and potentially con-flictive elements and flourishes not in spite of but thanks to difference and multiplicity. Consequently, harmony is con-stantly threatened by contention, discord, dissension, disso-nance, and strife. The union, order, beauty, and enjoyment that harmony produces are always precarious and require constant and assiduous cultivation. Finally, harmony is not merely an intellectual consensus but also a matter of the heart and action, of mutual love and effective solidarity. It is, in a nutshell, a way of life.

This harmony, according to the Vietnamese worldview, must be achieved at three levels. Basic to the Vietnamese worldview is what is called the three-element philosophy *(triet ly tam tai).* The three elements are Heaven *(thien* or *troi),* Earth *(dia* or *dat),* and Humanity *(nhan* or *nguoi),* which together constitute the whole of reality. Heaven refers to three distinct but related beings: (1) the visible

---

4. Franz-Josef Eilers, ed., *For All the Peoples of Asia: Federation of Asian Bishops' Conferences. Documents from 1992 to 1996,* vol. 2 (Quezon City, Philippines: Claretian, 1997), 232.

firmament above humans (as opposed to Earth); (2) the moral laws; and, most important, (3) the Creator, who is called *Ong Troi* (literally: Mr. Heaven), and is thought of in personal terms, endowed with intellect and will. The firmament is the place where the Creator dwells; the moral laws are the Creator's will and dispositions; and the Creator is the supreme being who is transcendent, omnipotent, and eternal and who actively governs and directs the world through providence.

Earth also refers to three distinct yet related things: (1) the material reality lying beneath humans (as opposed to Heaven above); (2) that which gives rise to entities composed of the five agents *(ngu hanh)* of metal, wood, water, fire, and earth; and (3) matter in general, which is essentially directed upward to Heaven.

Humanity refers to human beings "whose heads carry Heaven and whose feet trample upon Earth" *(dau doi troi, chan dap dat);* that is, humans are the link or union between Heaven and Earth. Humans express the power of Heaven and Earth by being "the sage inside and the king outside" *(noi thanh ngoai vuong),* that is, by orienting upward to Heaven *(tri tri;* literally: arriving at understanding) through knowing Heaven, trusting in Heaven, and acting out the will of Heaven on the one hand, and by orienting downward to Earth *(cach vat;* literally: examining all material things) through the use of material things for the benefit of all. As the hyphen connecting Heaven and Earth and as the microcosm, humans unite the male and the female, the positive and the negative, light and darkness, spirit and matter, the *yin* and the *yang.* They also combine the characteristics of the five agents: subtlety (water), strength (fire), vitality (wood), constancy (metal), and generosity (earth). In this way humans practice the human heart *(nhan tam)* and the human way *(nhan dao).*

The most important principle of the *tam tai* philosophy is that all three constitutive elements of reality are intrinsically connected with one another and mutually dependent. None can exist without the other two. Heaven without Earth and Humanity cannot produce or express anything. Earth without Heaven and Humanity would be an empty desert. Humanity without Heaven would be directionless, and without Earth, Humanity would have nowhere to exist and to act. Each of the three elements has its own function to perform: Heaven gives birth; Earth nurtures; and Humanity harmonizes *(thien sinh, dia duong, nhan hoa)*. Consequently, all human actions, to be successful and virtuous, must be governed by three principles: they must be carried out in accord with Heaven's will *(thien thoi)*, with the propitious favor of Earth *(dia loi)*, and for the harmony of Humanity *(nhan hoa)*.[5]

To Be Is To-Be-in-Harmony

This threefold harmony among Heaven, Earth, and Humanity is rooted in the harmony between two constitutive components within each of the three realities. Following the worldview expressed in the Book of Changes *(I Ching)*, one of the five Confucian classics, the Vietnamese see each reality as composed of two opposing elements known symbolically

---

5. This philosophy is claimed to be represented on the upper surface of the bronze drum, especially the one discovered at Ngoc Lu in 1901 and now preserved at the Center for Far-Eastern Antiquities *(Vien Dong Bac Co)* in Hanoi. This philosophy has been elaborated by Kim Dinh in his *Su Diep Trong Dong* (San Jose: Thanh Nien Quoc Gia, 1984). See also Vu Dinh Trac, "Triet ly truyen thong Viet Nam don duong cho Than Hoc Viet Nam," *Dinh Huong* 11 (1966): 23–47. Vu Dinh Trac believes that traditional Vietnamese philosophy is constituted by *tam tai* philosophy, yin-yang metaphysics, and agricultural philosophy. These three strands are illustrated by the various symbols on the upper surface of the Dong Son bronze drums.

as *yin* (Vietnamese: *am*) and *yang* (Vietnamese: *duong*). *Yang* stands for heaven, firmness, light, day, life, activity, masculinity, and *yin* for their corresponding opposites: earth, softness, darkness, night, death, receptivity, femininity. Of the five agents mentioned above, wood and fire belong to *yang*, and metal and water to *yin*, while earth belongs to both.

No reality is completely *yang*, and no reality is completely *yin*. As can be seen from the familiar representation of t'ai-chi, reality is pictured as a circle divided into two equal parts—one black, with a white dot in it (representing *yang*), and the other white, with a black dot in it (representing *yin*). *Yin* and *yang* are the two external and visible forces of the indivisible, invisible, transcendent, and absolute One that is the source of all reality. Though they are mutually opposing forces, *yin* and *yang* do not destroy each other but complement each other, because in the *yang* there is already the seed of *yin* (the white dot), and in the *yin* there is already the seed of *yang* (the black dot).

There is a law of reversal in the movement of *yin* and *yang:* when one reaches its highest point, it begins to descend, allowing the other to ascend; and when it reaches its lowest point, the other descends, allowing it to ascend. Thus there is always a balance or harmony in the universe, maintained by the One that is the Tao (Way). The Tao is the Third Principle or Force maintaining the two poles of *yin* and *yang* in balance and harmony. Humans must realize this harmony in their bodies to achieve good health (illness being the lack of balance among the various bodily components) and in their emotional and spiritual lives so as to be in harmony with each other, with Earth, and with Heaven.

This sense of harmony between the two opposing poles of reality is expressed in many popular proverbs and sayings: *Trong rui co may, trong may co rui* (There is bad luck in good luck, there is good luck in bad luck); *Trong do co den, trong den co do* (Red contains black, black contains red); *Khong ai giau ba ho, khong ai kho ba doi* (No one is wealthy for three families, no one is poor for three generations); *Bi cuc thai lai* (After extreme unhappiness happiness returns). It is also expressed in the Vietnamese custom of always giving gifts in pairs, such as two bottles of wine rather than one.

This sense of harmony and balance is expressed in the Vietnamese language, which always couples two antonyms together to express totality and wholeness: *troi dat* (heaven-earth), *song nui* (river-mountain), *song chet* (life-death), *ngay dem* (day-night), *sang toi* (morning-evening), *trai gai* (boy-girl), *nam nu* (man-woman), *chong vo* (husband-wife), *cha me* (father-mother). This harmony is also visible in the way many Vietnamese compound expressions can be reversed at will without any change in their meanings: *binh an* or *an binh* (peace), *trang nghiem* or *nghiem trang* (solemn). It is also embodied in the extremely common way in which the four words of two compound expressions are split and combined together to express a meaning: *dao vo nghia chong* (the duties of husband and wife). The two compound expressions are *dao nghia* (duties-obligations) and *vo chong* (wife-husband). While it is perfectly correct to say *dao nghia vo chong,* keeping the words of each compound expression together, it is better to split the two compound expressions and join the two first words of each compound expression *(dao* and *vo)* and connect the two last words of each compound expression *(nghia* and *chong)*. Thus, *dao vo nghia chong* (alternatively, *dao chong nghia vo*) expresses better the unity between "duties-obligations" and "wife-husband." This morphological structure that expresses balance and harmony is extremely common in the Vietnamese language and is unique to it.

To Be Is To-Be-in-Relationships

To achieve harmony among Heaven, Earth, and Humanity one must perform faithfully the duties of one's relationships with others, that is, with Heaven, Earth, and other human beings. Indeed, for the Vietnamese, to be is to-be-in-relationships, and to live morally is to determine one's position in this web of relationships and perform well the duties deriving from one's position.

The importance of discerning correctly one's relationship toward others is particularly evident in the ways the Vietnamese address each other. Strictly speaking, there are in the Vietnamese language no personal pronouns that do not express one's relationships with the addressee, unlike the English *I* and *you*. These are used for all kinds of subjects and objects irrespective of their personal relationships. A boy addresses his mother as "you," and refers to himself as "I," and uses the same pronouns when addressing his bullying classmate. In merely hearing "I" and "you," one does not know how they are related to each other.

By contrast, addressing another person, the Vietnamese have to determine his or her gender, age, rank, family and social relationships, the appropriate degree of respect and familiarity, and a host of other elements that make up the relationship between them and the addressee, and then use the correct form of address and self-referral to express their proper position and relationship to that person. Furthermore, these forms of address and self-referral change, even for the same person, depending on the emotional context. Different forms are used for the same person when speaking in love or in anger, for instance. The Vietnamese language is extremely complicated not only in its morphology and grammar but in the correct use of forms of address, for which there are no fixed rules, since they express one's ever-changing personal relationships with the people one converses with. Indeed, contrary to Descartes' "I think, therefore I am," the Vietnamese would say, "We are, therefore I am." In the Vietnamese culture, relationship is everything!

Relationships and Corresponding Duties and Obligations

Relationships are manifold, each with its attendant duties and obligations. In the second part of this chapter we examine how the Vietnamese view the relationships of humans with Heaven and Earth, especially in their religions. Here we discuss the relationships that humans have among themselves, in the family as well as in the society at large. In the Confucian tradition, the Vietnamese divide them into three bonds *(tam cuong)*—between king and subject, between husband and wife, between parent and child—each with its requisite virtue. Later, these relations are expanded to include those between siblings and between friends. Each member of the pair in the relationship has his or her proper obligation to perform toward the other, even though in practice the duty of the superior member is often presumed, and more emphasis is laid on that of the subordinate member. Thus, between king and subject, there must be loyalty *(trung);* between husband and wife, submission *(tong);* between parent and child, piety *(hieu);* between siblings, mutual yielding *(de);* and between friends, love-solidarity *(tinh).*

Besides these duties incumbent upon one's specific position, some of which we discuss in detail below, there are five virtues *(ngu thuong)* that must characterize one's dealings with all: *nhan* (compassion, benevolence, love for one's fellow human beings), *nghia* (justice, righteousness, sense of moral duty), *le* (propriety, social appropriateness), *tri* (knowledge, wisdom), and *tin* (sincerity, truthfulness). These five relationships with their respective obligations and these five virtues form the core of Vietnamese ethics and lie at the foundation of Vietnamese culture. They are the code or grammar of Vietnamese culture.

Harmony will be achieved in oneself, with one's superiors, with one's family, with one's fellows, with Earth and Heaven, only if one performs fully one's obligations and duties flowing from one's social and family position and practices the five virtues mentioned above.

Woman and Man: Basic Equality

Of the five relationships and their corresponding duties, two merit special consideration because of their large social and ethical implications for daily life, especially for Vietnamese expatriates. The first is that between husband and wife, and, more generally, between man and woman. As was mentioned in the previous chapter, the ancient Vietnamese family system was most likely matriarchal, with women ruling over the clan or tribe. Later, adopting the patriarchal system introduced by the Chinese, the Vietnamese began to favor the male and disparage the female. In terms of progeny, a son is said to be worth ten daughters. The woman is said to be governed by three submissions *(tam tong):* when unmarried, she is subjected to her father; when married, to her husband; and when widowed, to her son. The four virtues *(tu duc)* judged to be proper to her are predominantly home-related: *cong* (domestic skills), *dung* (demure manners), *ngon* (respectful speech), and *hanh* (virtuous behavior).

While this patriarchal system, derived from Neo-Confucian ethics, was promoted by the upper class and the literati, it was not able to dislodge the Vietnamese women from their relatively high position in the family and society, especially among the peasants and the lower classes. Indeed, in the 1930s, there was an influential literary movement inspired by the French Enlightenment called *Tu Luc Van Doan* (Self-Reliance Literary Group), which by means of periodicals and novels sought to abolish customs and practices detrimental to the dignity of woman, such as arranged marriage and the harsh treatment of daughters-in-law, and to promote individual freedom and autonomy.

In contrast to Chinese culture, the Vietnamese culture and legal codes accord many rights and privileges to women, and many Vietnamese proverbs and popular songs emphasize the basic equality between man and woman and the need for mutual support and love between husband and wife. Indeed, popular wisdom considers the role of the mother more important and difficult than that of the father: *Cha sinh khong tay me duong* (The father's giving life is not equal to the mother's nurturing), and *Cha chet an com voi ca, me chet liem la dau cho* (If your father dies, you can still eat rice and fish; if your mother dies, you will have to lick leaves at the market). Perhaps because of this egalitarian tradition, Vietnamese women have found it easier to adapt to the American way of life than Vietnamese men.

Filial Piety

The second relationship that deserves special consideration is that between parent and child, and its concomitant duty of filial piety. Just as charity or love plays a central role in Christian ethics, so filial piety lies at the basis of Vietnamese moral and religious life. Piety toward one's parents requires reverence for and obedience to them and taking attentive care of them when they are still alive, especially in their sickness and old age. Another sacred duty is to provide them with progeny, especially male ones, so their lineage and names may be perpetuated. After their deaths, veneration and sacrifices must be offered to them on specific occasions, as will be shown in our discussion of the cult of ancestors in the following chapter.

Vietnamese folklore is replete with stories of children sacrificing their own happiness for their parents, at times going to absurd lengths, such as a son who let mosquitoes bite him rather than his mother. Perhaps the most famous is that of Chu Dong Tu, whose family was so poor that he had only one loincloth.When his mother died, he used it to bury her with, and therefore could not go out of the house except at night. Eventually, as a reward for his filial piety, he was married to a princess. Another paragon of filial piety is presented in the masterpiece of Vietnamese literature, Nguyen Du's epic, *Doan Truong Tan Thanh*, more popularly known as *Truyen Kieu*, whose heroine Thuy Kieu sold herself into prostitution in order to buy her jailed father's freedom.[6]

Filial piety is an expression of gratitude for parents' immense love and care for their offspring. An oft-cited proverb says: *Cong cha nhu nui Thai Son, nghia me nhu nuoc song Nguon chay ra* (The father's labor [merit] is as high as Mount Thai Son, the mother's love is as deep as River Nguon flowing from its source). Vietnamese are taught that *mot long tho me kinh cha, cho tron chu hieu moi la dao con* (respect and honor your mother and father, thus you will fulfill the obligations of filial piety derived from the way of being an offspring). *Dao con,* which requires *dao hieu* (filial piety), literally means the "way" or "religion" of being a son or a daughter.

Vietnamese Religions

As has been said above, the Vietnamese people see human persons as constituted by relationships not only

---

6. Nguyen Du (1765–1820) is universally regarded as the greatest Vietnamese poet. For an English translation of this epic, see *The Tale of Kieu,* trans. Huynh Sanh Thong (New Haven, CT: Yale University Press, 1983).

---

among themselves but also between them and Heaven and Earth. These latter relationships are lived out in religions. The Vietnamese often refer to Three Religions *(tam giao)*, that is, Buddhism, Confucianism, and Taoism. These religions are not native to Vietnam but are foreign imports—just like Christianity. However, these religions did not come to Vietnam as to an empty desert; they encountered there an indigenous religion. This religion was not swallowed up by them. Rather, it absorbed and in the process transformed them, just as they too transformed it. Furthermore, the Three Religions—and to a much lesser extent, Christianity—have become so much part and parcel of the Vietnamese culture that it is impossible to say exactly where Vietnamese religions begin and where they end with respect to the Vietnamese culture. Here we examine the Vietnamese indigenous religions and the Three Religions, postponing consideration of Christianity until chapter 7.

The Way of Heaven (Dao Tho Troi)

Together with *dao hieu* (the way or religion of filial piety), *dao tho troi* (the way or religion of worshiping Heaven), or *thien dao* (the way of Heaven), constitutes the core of Vietnamese indigenous religious beliefs. The former is practiced in the veneration of ancestors (which will be discussed in the following chapter), and the latter in the ancient ritual of the Sacrifice at the South Gate offered by the emperor *(Te Nam Giao)* and in the faithful execution of Heaven's will by all, especially by the emperor or king who is considered the Son of Heaven *(thien tu)*.

In Vietnamese, there are two series of words for "God." One is composed of Sino-Vietnamese words: *Thuong De* (Ruler on high, supreme ruler), *Thien* (Heaven), *Thien Chua* or *Thien Chu* (Lord of Heaven), or simply *Chua* (Lord). The other series consists of pure Vietnamese words: *Troi* (Heaven), more commonly, *Ong Troi* (Mr. Heaven), and sometimes *Ong Thanh* (Mr. Blue Heaven). Today, Vietnamese Christians use *Chua, Thien Chua,* and *Duc Chua Troi* (*Duc* is an honorific title meaning "Noble" or "Venerable").

In proverbs and popular songs, there are many references to *Troi* and *Ong Troi*. They express the most fundamental beliefs of the Vietnamese people about God. First of all, Heaven (not the blue firmament) is a supreme personal entity designated by the title *Ong* (mister), endowed with intellect and will, with whom one can converse and to whom one can pray for favors. A very popular folksong is a prayer addressed by the common people to Heaven:

> *Lay Troi mua xuong* (Heaven, please send down the rains)
> *Lay nuoc toi uong* (So I may have water to drink)
> *Lay ruong toi cay* (So I can plow my fields)
> *Lay bat com day* (So my rice bowl will be full)
> *Lay khuc ca to* (So the fish I catch will be big).

Heaven is confessed to be the Creator who directs, protects, and nurtures all created things with his all-knowing and all-wise providence so that all things may move harmoniously:

> *Troi sinh, Troi duong* (Heaven creates, Heaven nurtures).
> *Troi sinh voi, Troi sinh co* (Heaven creates elephants, Heaven creates grass).
> *Cha me sinh con, Troi sinh tinh* (Parents give birth to their children, Heaven gives them their character).

Heaven is just, is partial to no one, sees the hearts of people, and rewards and punishes them according to their desserts:

Troi co mat (Heaven has eyes).
Khong co troi ai o voi ai (Without Heaven, whom can you live with?).
Phi cua Troi, muoi doi chang co (Waste Heaven's gifts, and you won't have them for ten generations).
Biet su Troi, muoi doi chang kho (Know Heaven's will, and you won't suffer for ten generations).
Che cua nao, Troi trao cua ay (What you spurn, Heaven gives you).

Heaven is kind and loving, even in punishing:

Troi danh con tranh bua an (Heaven avoids striking you during your meals).

The words with which the famous Nguyen Du ends his celebrated 3,252-verse epic summarize well the Vietnamese beliefs in Heaven:

Ngam hay muon su tai tro (Know that all things depend on Heaven),
troi kia da bat lam nguoi co than (Heaven has assigned to each person a position).
Bat phong tran phai phong tran (If your lot is to roll in dust, you will roll in dust),
cho thanh cao moi duoc phan thanh cao (If you are given a high position, you will sit on high).
Co dau thien vi nguoi nao (Heaven is partial to no one),
chu tai chu menh doi dao ca hai (Heaven does not bestow talent and good fortune to anyone at the same time).

> *Co tai ma cay chi tai* (If you have talents, do not take
>   pride in them),
> *chu tai lien voi chu tai mot van* (For talent and disas-
>   ter rhyme together).
> *Da mang lay nghiep vao than* (Each of us carries his
>   or her own karma),
> *cung dung trach lan troi gan troi xa* (Then do not
>   reproach Heaven for being near or far).
> *Thien can o tai long ta* (The root of goodness lies in
>   our heart),
> *chu tam kia moi bang ba chu tai* (The heart is worth
>   three times talent).

In sum, for the Vietnamese, Heaven is the personal, transcendent yet immanent, benevolent yet just God, the creator
of the universe, source of all life, and supreme judge.

Even though the Vietnamese common people believe in
and venerate Heaven, there are no rituals, private or public,
by which they express these feelings toward Heaven. Only
the emperor or king, who alone carries the title of *Son of
Heaven,* performs the *Te Nam Giao* (*te* means sacrifice; *nam*
means the south, the direction of light; *giao* means encounter,
the meeting between Heaven and Heaven's children). Once a
year, and later once every three years, the king, on New Year's
Day of the lunar calendar, after due purification and fasting,
offered a solemn sacrifice to Heaven in the name of the
people, invoking Heaven's blessings on the nation. During the
last dynasty (the Nguyen), the sacrifice, which had to be performed according to detailed instructions, took place at the
South Gate of the capital city of Hue on a raised four-level
hill. The highest level is round, 42 meters in diameter, representing Heaven; the two lower levels are square, one 85
meters, the other 165 meters in length, symbolizing Earth;
and the lowest level is rectangular, 265 meters in width and

390 meters in length. The *Te Nam Giao* represents the most solemn expression of the Vietnamese people's faith in God as creator and ruler of the universe.

Vietnamese Confucianism

It is into this indigenous religious world that the Three Religions entered Vietnam. As mentioned in the previous chapter, during the Chinese domination, Confucianism, which originated from Confucius or K'ung Fu-Tzu (551–487 BC), was imposed on Vietnam, especially from the third century AD. Even after Vietnam regained independence in the tenth century, Confucianism (or more precisely, the Neo-Confucianism of the Sung [960–1279] and Ming [1368–1644] dynasties) continued to dominate all aspects of Vietnamese life, particularly family and social relations. Confucianism (Vietnamese: *Nho giao*) enjoyed the status of state orthodoxy, especially under the Early Tran, Later Le, and Nguyen dynasties, when the Confucian classics, namely, the Five Classics (the Books of Poetry, Rites, History, Spring and Autumn, and Changes) and the Four Books *(Mencius, Great Learning, Doctrine of the Mean,* and *The Analects),* were adopted as the basis for individual education and as standard texts for the preparation of government functionaries (the mandarins).

Confucianism is more an ethico-political system than a religion in the Western sense of the term. Essentially a humanism, it strongly asserts the centrality of humanity and human values, affirms the native goodness of human nature, and promotes the cultivation of virtues. The fundamental virtue is *nhan* (humanity, humanness, benevolence), which includes among other virtues that of reciprocity (do not do to others what you would not have them do to you). To achieve *nhan,* one has to know the will of Heaven, and since Heaven acts in history, one can discover Heaven's will by studying the past embodied in traditions, literature, rites, and music.

Another way to practice *nhan* is to know one's correct name *(chinh danh)*, that is, one's position and relation in the family and in society, and as a result, practice in an appropriate manner the three bonds *(tam cuong)* and five virtues *(ngu thuong)* mentioned above. The goal of moral self-cultivation is to become a *quan tu* (gentleman, superior man), who, in contrast to the *tieu nhan* (little man), does things because of their intrinsic rightness and not for profit.

Confucianism encourages the performance of traditional rites as a way to perfect human moral nature. For example, it promotes the veneration of ancestors in order to practice filial piety and to emulate the virtues of the dead, even though the common people attach religious meanings to them. As for the worship of Confucius himself, in AD 59, Emperor Han Ming Ti made Confucianism official state orthodoxy, proclaimed Confucius patron of scholars, and ordered sacrifices to be offered to him. This practice was also adopted by Vietnam. In Hanoi there is a magnificent shrine called *Van Mieu* (Temple of Literature), where Confucius and his disciples are venerated.

Even though, as has been pointed out in the previous chapter, state examinations on the Confucian texts and the use of Chinese characters were abolished in Vietnam at the beginning of the twentieth century, Confucianism as an ethics-religious system is still deeply influential among the Vietnamese whose "Confucian DNA" remains permanent in spite of the political, social, and religious changes that have taken place in their country.

Vietnamese Taoism

Taoism (Vietnamese: *Lao giao* or *Dao giao*) is both a philosophical system and a religious practice. The former is rational, contemplative, and nonsectarian, and accepts death as a natural event, while the latter is magical, cultic, esoteric, and sectarian, and attempts to achieve immortality by means of alchemy. Both branches were imported to Vietnam at the same time as Confucianism.

Philosophically, Taoism is based on the writings attributed to Lao Tzu (the *Tao Te Ching*), Chuang Tzu, and Huai Nan Tzu. Central to its teaching is the doctrine concerning Tao (the Way). As the unmanifest, absolute, unchanging, and transcendent source of all things, Tao is called nonbeing *(vo)*. But as manifested in creation, through *yin* and *yang*, it is called being *(huu)* and is active in the phenomenal, relative, and ever-changing world. Furthermore, as has been explained above, the two polar opposites of *yang* and *yin* move through the five agents—water, wood, fire, earth, and metal—according to the law of reversal and complement each other.

In contrast to Confucianism, which promotes continuous efforts at moral self-cultivation and just governance of the state, Taoism espouses nonaction or noncontrivance *(vo vi)* on the personal and social levels, which does not mean doing nothing but rather following the Tao, that is, acting according to the inclination of nature, as spontaneously as water flowing downward and fire rising upward.

Religiously, Taoism conceives the universe as populated by a vast array of forces, organized into a hierarchy. At the top of the hierarchy is, of course, Tao; below Tao is the primordial chaos; and below chaos are the three officials called the Three Heavenly Worthies. Below them is a vast multitude of spirits, demons, ghosts, and supernatural animals. The same energies of *yin* and *yang* and the five agents are at work on all levels. The human body is believed to be a microcosm, reflecting the cosmic hierarchy. The goal of Taoism as a religious practice is maintaining in one's body the harmony, creativity, and order of the unmanifest Tao that operates in the macrocosm and in this way becoming immortal beings *(tien)*.

The techniques for achieving immortality include diet (eating foods that nourish the five organs—lung, heart, spleen, liver, kidneys—corresponding to the five agents), gymnastic exercises that assist the circulation of energies through the body and eliminate internal obstructions, deep and controlled breathing, sexual techniques preventing the loss of semen, the use of elixirs, and the practice of morally good deeds and attitudes such as humility, impartiality, and control over the passions.

While both branches of Taoism are influential in Vietnam, it is the religious current that is the more popular. Its hierarchy of heavenly beings fits in well with the animist worldview of the Vietnamese indigenous religion. Furthermore, Taoist priests fulfill sacred functions that respond to the daily needs of people such as exorcism, healing, divination, petition for public and personal welfare, prayers and offerings to the dead, and the making of talismans and charms. Needless to say, religious Taoism is very popular among the less educated and poor Vietnamese.

Vietnamese Buddhism

Originating from the Indian prince Siddhartha Gautama, also known as Šakyamuni (560–480 BC), who after a prolonged regimen of ascetic practices and meditation, attained awakening or enlightenment (hence, his title *the Buddha*), Buddhism soon spread from the Indian subcontinent to other countries of South, Southeast, and Northwest Asia, including Sri Lanka, Burma, Thailand, China, Vietnam, Korea, Japan, and Tibet.

The Buddha's enlightenment is formulated in the Four Noble Truths that summarize the Buddhist interconnected insights into the human condition. The first truth affirms the universal fact of suffering (description of the symptom), the second the cause of suffering (diagnosis), the third the overcoming of suffering (prognosis), and the fourth the way of overcoming suffering (prescription). Suffering can be of mind or body and is the sign that existence is characterized by unsatisfactoriness or dis-ease. The cause of suffering is craving which, together with lust and greed, keeps the person attached to transitory existence. The remedy for suffering is the cessation of craving or detachment from craving, which leads to liberation. The path leading from ignorance to enlightenment, from suffering to liberation or Nirvana is the Eightfold Path. This Eightfold Path is a middle way between the two extremes of self-indulgence and self-mortification and consists in eight related (though not successive) practices. These eight practices may be divided into three categories: moral conduct (right speech, right action, right livelihood); mental discipline (right effort, right mindfulness, right concentration); and intuitive wisdom (right understanding, right thought).

In addition to these Four Noble Truths, Buddhism incorporates two principal doctrines of Hinduism, namely, karma (fruits of action) and samsara (rebirth). According to the first doctrine, every thought or deed produces karma, which may be good or evil. According to the second, a living being will undergo repeated rebirths and assume a different form in each rebirth according to the karma of the past. In Buddhism there are five states of existence, the two good states being deity and humanity, and the three bad ones being animal, hungry ghost, and denizen of hell. The Eightfold Path is designed to help humans achieve the difficult and long process of liberation from the cycle of rebirths and reach Nirvana. Nirvana is of two kinds: Nirvana with a residue and Nirvana without a residue. The former can be achieved in this life, for example, by the Buddha, when the cravings that lead to continued rebirths are extinguished but the five aggregates making up human existence (i.e., matter, sensation, perception, predisposition, and consciousness) are still present. The latter, called *parinirvana,* is achieved only after death, and about this the Buddha, when asked to say what it is, answered with silence.

After the death of the Buddha, Buddhism soon split into two major groups. One, known as Theravada (the Way of the Elders) Buddhism, adheres strictly to the teaching of the Buddha as expounded above, stresses the humanity of Gautama the Buddha, and holds that the path to Nirvana, in principle open to all Buddhists, is in practice possible only to monks and nuns who alone can become *arhant,* that is, the saintly sage.

The followers of Mahayana (the Great Vehicle) Buddhism found such a view of Nirvana too restrictive and even the ideal of the *arhant,* intent on his or her own liberation, too selfish and individualistic. In contrast to Theravada Buddhism, which it characterizes using the pejorative term of *Hanayana* (the small, lesser vehicle), Mahayana Buddhism holds that every sentient being possesses the Buddha nature and is therefore capable of attaining Buddhahood. The way to become a Buddha is made easier, not through strenuous asceticism but through faith and devotion to the Buddha and compassion for all living beings. Furthermore, it develops the ideal of the bodhisattva, that is, a being who, though already enlightened, delays the final entry into Nirvana until every sentient being is saved from this world of suffering. Lastly, Mahayana Buddhism emphasizes that all reality, including Nirvana itself, is "empty" (*sunya*), that is to say, no reality, down to its irreducible ultimate components *(dharma),* possesses its own existence or self-nature because it depends on causes and conditions other than itself for its existence.

Both branches of Buddhism entered Vietnam first from India (Theravada) and later from China (Mahayana) in the first century AD. From China, two forms of Buddhism were imported: Zen (Vietnamese: *thien*), which emphasizes meditation as a way to achieve enlightenment and the importance of ordinary tasks of the present moment, and Pure Land (Vietnamese: *Tinh Do*), which stresses faith in the Buddha Amitabha (Immeasurable Light), the recitation of his name, and the religious goal of being reborn in his "Pure Land" or "Western Paradise." One extremely popular Buddha in Vietnamese Buddhism is Quan Am Thi Kinh, the Vietnamese female figure corresponding to the Indian male Avalokitesvara, or the Buddha of Compassion, who vows to postpone his own freedom from suffering until all other beings are saved. We discuss the role of Quan Am Thi Kinh in the following chapter.

Buddhism achieved social and political preeminence during the eleventh through the thirteenth centuries under the Ly and Tran dynasties, but thereafter experienced a long decline as Confucianism was granted the status of state orthodoxy. It was not until 1951 that the General Association of Buddhists (Tong Hoi Phat Giao) was established to unite all the different branches of Vietnamese Buddhism, and later, in 1963, the Buddhist Institute for the Promotion of the Faith (Vien Hoa Dao) was founded. During the Vietnam War, under the Catholic president Ngo Dinh Diem, Buddhists agitated against religious restrictions by the government. On June 11, 1963, a Buddhist monk, Thich Quang Duc, burned himself to death in protest, and his self-immolation was followed by those of some thirty others, both monks and nuns. Under the communist government since 1975, Buddhism, like other religious organizations, experienced opposition and restrictions.

Among contemporary Buddhist monks who have attracted a large following, even among non-Vietnamese, Thich Nhat Hanh (1926–) is without doubt the most well known not only because of his activities during the Vietnam War but also through his many publications and the Plump Village in southern France that he founded as a retreat center. His teaching on interbeing (i.e., all beings are interdependent) and mindfulness in the Zen tradition and his brand of Engaged Buddhism are very favorably received.

Other Religions in Vietnam

Besides these three imported religions, there are other religions, with a much smaller number of followers, that were founded by the Vietnamese themselves. Among these two deserve a brief mention. The first is *Dao Cao Dai*. Its full name is *Dai Dao Tam Ky Pho Do* (the Great Religion of the Third Dispensation of Salvation). The term *Cao Dai* literally means "high tower" or "elevated palace" and by metonymy designates God ("the Most High"). Caodaism represents a syncretistic attempt to unite the *Tam Giao* with Western religious elements, in particular, Roman Catholicism.

Caodaism was founded by Ngo Van Chieu, who claimed in 1919 to have received a message during a seance that God would make himself known with a new name, Cao Dai. He was soon joined by converts, among whom the most important was Pham Cong Tac, who became the leader. In 1926 the new religion was recognized by the French colonial government with the center in Tay Ninh, where a magnificent temple was built the following year.

Fundamental to Caodaism is the belief in the one God, the Most High, creator of all things. The symbol of Caodaist monotheism is the One Eye, which is reminiscent of Freemasonry. Moreover, the one God is professed to be the savior of all things. He carries out his saving work *(Pho Do)* by communicating the Great Doctrine *(Dai Dao)* in three dispensations or stages *(Tam Ky).*

In the first stage, the Most High bestowed his universal self-revelation to all peoples; however, this revelation was not well preserved and transmitted due to the lack of proper mediation. In the second dispensation, the Most High communicated the Great Doctrine in five branches: *Nho Dao* (Confucianism), *Than Dao* (Vietnamese animism), *Thanh Dao* (Christianity), *Tien Dao* (Taoism), and *Phat Dao* (Buddhism). In Caodaism, the third and last dispensation, the Most High wishes to unite all religions and communicates his truths and his designs no longer by means of intermediaries but directly, through spiritistic seances.

Caodaism thus presents itself as the unification of all religions, both Eastern and Western. On the one hand, it adopts many of the elements of the three traditional Vietnamese religions, Buddhism, Confucianism, and Taoism. For instance, from Buddhism it takes over the doctrine of karma and reincarnation; from Confucianism, it derives much of its individual, family, and social ethics; and from Taoism, it adopts many of its rituals. Even in its organization, it stipulates that beneath the pope there be three representatives *(chuong phap)* from each of the three religions whose task is to examine the pronouncements of the pope, correct him if necessary, and approve the books of prayers and doctrines for publication.

On the other hand, Caodaism appropriates the Western theosophist practice of spiritism and makes it one of its principal means to obtain divine revelation. It also adopts much of the terminology of the Roman Catholic Church's sacramental and canonical system (e.g., pope, cardinal, archbishop, bishop, priest, deacon).

Ethically, Caodaism urges simplicity of life, mutual charity, and social responsibility. Furthermore, it promotes a strict ethical code. Minimally, all the faithful must abstain from the five prohibitions (no killing of any kind, stealing, sexual improprieties, drinking, and lying) and observe the four commandments (obedience to the superior, humility, financial honesty, and respect for all).

The second Vietnamese newer religion is *Phat Giao Hoa Hao* (Hoa Hoa Buddhism). Its founder is Huynh Phu So (1919–47). Like the founder of Caodaism, Huynh Phu So was born in South Vietnam. In 1937, on a summer night during a thunderstorm, he had a dramatic religious experience and felt called to found a new religion that would unite the three imported religions (without Christianity, unlike Caodaism). The basic religion would be Buddhism, but in a reformed state, and the name given to it, *Hoa Hao,* is the name of the founder's village, which means "peace and goodness." Huynh Phu So was murdered by the Communists on March 17, 1947, and his body was thrown into a river.

Phat Giao Hoa Hao follows the same doctrines and moral practices as those of Buddhism. What is new is its insistence on simplicity in rituals. It eliminates practices that smack of superstition such as the offering of meat, glutinous rice, and other votive objects to the dead, sorcery, divination, seances, and the use of amulets. It also removes statues of the Buddha, the bodhisattvas, spirits, and genies from the pagodas. Prayers are said by the whole assembly of the faithful without accompanying music, bells, and wooden knockers.

The Unity of All Religions

As is clear from this survey of the two most recent Vietnamese religions, there is a strong tendency among the Vietnamese to unify all religions. This is particularly true with regard to Buddhism, Confucianism, and Taoism, which the Vietnamese often refer to as *tam giao dong nguyen,* literally, "three religions with the same principle or origin."

Furthermore, the matrix that binds these three religions together and at the same time transforms them, making them "Vietnamese," is the original Vietnamese indigenous religion with its two basic characteristics, namely, belief in Heaven and filial piety.

There is a common Vietnamese saying that states that *dao nao cung tot* (all religions are good). This dictum should not be taken as espousing religious indifference in the sense that all religions are equally true and therefore it does not matter which religion one follows. Rather, it affirms the existence of good elements in all religions and therefore one should respect and learn from any one of them. In this sense, all Vietnamese, including Christians, are to some extent Buddhist, Confucianist, and Taoist since these religions have permeated the Vietnamese culture and way of life. It is extremely difficult if not impossible to determine the exact number of Buddhists, Confucianists, and Taoists among the Vietnamese population. All Vietnamese, if asked, would confess that they believe in Heaven and practice ancestor worship. This fact, which embodies the Vietnamese ideal of harmony, should be kept in mind when trying to understand Vietnamese culture and religious traditions.

Chapter 3

HOW DO THE VIETNAMESE CELEBRATE?

VIETNAMESE FEASTS AND CUSTOMS

As we have seen, culture is made up of four components: things (culture as material), meanings (culture as ideational), activities (culture as performance), and the code by which these things, meanings, and activities are expressed (culture as code). In the previous chapter we examined the meanings and the code of the Vietnamese culture, components that are difficult to grasp. In this chapter we look at some of its things and activities by focusing on key Vietnamese feasts and customs.

Foreigners usually take delight in sharing these things and activities, such as eating Vietnamese foods, wearing Vietnamese clothes (especially the *ao dai,* the much-admired woman's form-fitting dress, with long tight sleeves and with two panels at the waist, extending front and back to cover the loose, flowing pants), listening to Vietnamese music, looking at Vietnamese arts and architecture, participating in festivals and religious celebrations, and so forth. No doubt, these things and activities provide an easy entry into the Vietnamese culture, and from a practical standpoint, to appreciate the Vietnamese culture, it is more helpful to begin by sharing the lives of the Vietnamese in this way than by reflecting on Vietnamese philosophy and religions.

Religious Celebrations

Religious traditions enact their myths and beliefs in rituals and liturgical worship, and Vietnamese religions are no exception, as each of them has its own forms of worship and sacred celebrations. Furthermore, these rituals are often connected with important events in the life cycle, from birth to death, as well as with the seasonal changes of time and nature. Of course, it is impossible nor is it necessary to describe all the celebrations and festivals of the Vietnamese religions. I focus on those that are still widely practiced today, especially in the Vietnamese communities in the Diaspora.

Ancestor Veneration

Enter any Vietnamese home and you will often see in the most prominent corner of the living room an altar on which pictures of the ancestors are displayed, together with some offerings such as joss sticks, flowers, and fruits. Catholics most likely will place this altar beneath the one dedicated to God, Mary, and the saints.

Perhaps no other religious practice unites the Vietnamese people, irrespective of their faiths, more than ancestor veneration or worship. In Vietnamese it is called *dao tho ong ba* (literally: religion that worships the ancestors). The expressions *religion* and *worship* as well as the various practices associated with them were scandalous to Christian missionaries, especially in China and Vietnam, since to them they represented rank superstition. As a result, ancestor veneration was condemned by the Catholic Church, especially by Pope Benedict XIV in his apostolic constitution *Ex quo singulari* in 1742, in what is known as the Chinese

Rites Controversy. It was not until 1939 that the cult to Confucius and the ancestors was permitted on the grounds that it does not have a religious character but is a "merely civil and political" act.

In retrospect, the condemnation of ancestor veneration was a tragic mistake and a disaster for the Church in Asia, as many Asians, especially the eldest sons, refused to convert to Christianity because it was seen as a foreign religion that prohibited what was most sacred and religious in their cultures. Indeed, during the persecution of Vietnamese Catholics in the nineteenth century, there was a slogan to rally the people, *"binh Tay sat ta"*—literally, destroy the West and kill the evil religion (that is, Christianity), "evil" because it forbade among other things ancestor worship.

It is to be noted that the Vietnamese word *tho* does not necessarily have the connotation of adoration, which is reserved only for God. Rather, the compound expression *tho kinh* (or, characteristically, its reverse, *kinh tho*) means venerate-respect. In Vietnamese there is no strict distinction, as in Catholic theology, between adoration (which is reserved exclusively for God) and veneration (which is given to the saints). However, veneration of ancestors is not for the Vietnamese a "merely civil and political act," devoid of religious significance, as it is alleged in Vatican documents. On the contrary, it is the most religious and sacred act that a Vietnamese can perform.

Ancestor veneration or worship is rooted in a deep sense of gratitude to those who, with immense sacrifices, have given life to their children and nurtured them. The children then have the sacred obligation to love and respect their parents in return. The following folksong strongly urges them to fulfill the duties of filial piety:

> *Cong danh hai chu to mo* (If you do not succeed well
>   in your profession),
> *Lay gi khuya som phung tho to tien* (What will you
>   have to offer to your ancestors morning and
>   evening?)
> *Khon ngoan nho duc cha ong* (If you grow wise, it's
>   due to the merits of your parents).
> *Lam nen phai doai to tong phung tho* (If you have a
>   successful career, remember to worship your
>   ancestors).
> *Dao lam con cho hung ho* (Do not neglect your obli-
>   gations of filial duty),
> *Phai dem hieu kinh ma tho trang nghiem* (Rather, you
>   must venerate your ancestors in all seriousness).
> *Tu dau cho bang tu nha* (Nowhere is better than home
>   to be a religious),
> *Tho cha kinh me, ay la chan tu* (Venerate the father and
>   respect the mother, that is being a true religious).

Since "the father's labor is a mountain as high as Heaven and the mother's love is as deep as the waters of the Eastern Sea" *(cong cha nhu nui ngat troi, nghia me nhu nuoc o ngoai bien dong)*, a plethora of Vietnamese proverbs and folksongs reminds the Vietnamese children of the near-impossibility of repaying adequately the debt they owe their parents:

> *Bao gio ca ly hoa long* (Not until the samlet becomes
>   a dragon),
> *Den on cha me am bong ngay xua* (Will you repay in
>   full your parents' loving care for you).

Since a full repayment cannot be made during parents' life-times, it must continue after their deaths in the form of ancestor veneration as part of filial piety. Physically, filial piety requires that one do what one can to have progeny, preferably a male son, to continue the family lineage. Morally, it consists in avoiding any behavior that may bring dishonor to their name; more positively, it requires that children do well in their personal lives and careers so as to bring honor to parents. Ritually, ancestor worship consists in making offerings in the form of drinks, cooked foods, fruits, and other things as a sign of gratitude and love, on various occasions as will be mentioned below (the Vietnamese word for this act is *cung* or *te*).

Ancestor veneration is predicated on the belief that the dead survive in some form and, more importantly, do not cease to be involved with this world, especially their family, over which they continue to exercise protection. Their presence is invoked especially on the anniversaries of their deaths. In Vietnam, most people do not celebrate the anniversaries of their births (though the Western custom of celebrating birthdays is gaining favor, particularly among the young and the expatriates). Rather, it is the person's death that is commemorated by her or his descendants. On this day, called *ngay gio* (the forty-ninth and hundredth days after a person's death are the most solemn), all the children of the deceased and their families gather together, make offerings to the dead *(cung)*, pray for their protection, and eat a festive meal during which the food offerings are consumed. Catholics would also ask a Mass to be said for the deceased.

In ancient Vietnam, after the parents die, if the family is wealthy, an ancestral home called *tu duong* would be established and proceeds from a piece of land called *huong hoa* (literally: incense and fire) would be used to cover the costs of ancestor veneration. In older days, there was the custom, now almost universally abandoned, of burning paper money or even paper miniature houses in the belief that the dead may need them. On death anniversaries today the family goes to visit the tomb and makes sure that it is in good and clean condition. In Vietnam, proper maintenance of the tombs is a very grave duty.

In addition to the annual commemoration of the ancestors' deaths, there is also a religious function called *le cao gia tien* (literally: ceremony to inform the ancestors), which also includes offerings to the dead. The ancestors are informed of various important events in the family such as the birth of a child, the child's first month and first year, the passing of an examination, marriage, acquisition of a new house, or grave sickness and misfortune, or they are thanked or asked to provide protection, as appropriate.

Finally, in connection with the ancestors, there is a custom called *huy ky* (avoid and fear). While in the West it is a sign of affection to give to one's child the name of one's parents, in Vietnam it is strictly taboo to do so. The names of ancestors are considered sacred. One must avoid pronouncing them and giving their children these names.

Buddhist Festivals and Devotions

Among the many Buddhist festivals and devotions, one bears a striking resemblance to All Souls' Day in the Catholic liturgical calendar. It is known as *Vu Lan* (Wandering Souls' Day), which takes place on the full moon day of the seventh lunar calendar. On this day, prayers and offerings of foods and gifts are made at home and in the temples for the wandering souls of those who have died a tragic death or who have died childless so that there is no one to remember them. The famous poet Nguyen Du has composed a moving *Call to Wandering Souls (Van Chieu Hon,* also known as *Van Te Thap Loai Chung Sinh)* that has been compared to Thomas Gray's *Elegy Written in a Country Churchyard*. His prayer is that "Buddha, the compassionate, may grant them salvation, deliver them of their suffering, and lead them to the promised Western Paradise."

As mentioned in the previous chapter, one Buddhist devotion finds great favor among the Vietnamese, and that is the devotion to Quan Am Thi Kinh, the female Buddha of Compassion. Thi Kinh is supposed to be the name of a girl who was married to a poor peasant. One day, as her husband was asleep, she noticed a stray hair on his face and took a knife to remove it. He suddenly woke up and accused her of wanting to kill him. Thi Kinh did not vindicate herself and her silence was taken as an admission of guilt. Cast out of her home, she decided to find peace in a Buddhist monastery, but to be a monk she had to disguise herself as a man. A girl in the village fell in love with her, thinking she was a man, but she was rebuffed by Thi Kinh. Out of desperation, the girl gave herself to a man, became pregnant, gave birth to a son, carried him to the monastery, and accused Thi Kinh of being the father. Thi Kinh was brought in front of the community to defend herself, but before she could speak, the child screamed in the basket. She bent down and picked him up, and the gesture was taken as confirmation that she was his mother. Expelled from the community, she led a beggar's life to take care of the child. At her death, her true identity was discovered, and because of her tender mercy and forgiving soul, she was made a Buddha. Her statue as a woman carrying an infant in her arm is given a place of honor in every pagoda, and she is invoked as the compassionate protectress of children and all victims of misfortune and injustice.

Cultural Feasts and Customs

Visitors to Vietnam often marvel at the great numbers of festivals not only at the national but also the local level.

Not only national heroes whose names we mentioned in the first chapter are celebrated with great solemnity, but almost every village and county also celebrates their own protecting genii and founders and each profession its "patron saint." But among Vietnamese feasts and customs, none can match the celebrations of New Year of the lunar calendar, which is New Year, Independence Day, Thanksgiving Day, and Christmas rolled into one!

Tet Nguyen Dan

Tet Nguyen Den is the modified pronunciation of *tiet* (season), *nguyen* (beginning), and *dan* (morning). Commonly it is known simply as Tet. In older times, it lasted a whole month; then it was reduced to a week; today it is three days long. Some seven days before Tet, there is a ceremony to dispatch the god Earth *(Ong Tao)* to Heaven so he can make a report of what has transpired during the passing year. On New Year's Eve, at midnight, there is a ceremony called *Giao Thua* to send away the old year and welcome the new one. Sacrifices and offerings are made to the ancestors, asking them to come back to the family for celebrations. Everyone must return home to be with their loved ones. All debts must be paid, all offenses forgiven, all hostilities ceased (that is why the Communists' Tet Offensive against South Vietnam in 1968 was regarded as not only a military atrocity but also a sacrilege). Customarily, the first day is spent with the paternal family, the second day with the maternal family, and the third day with friends. Children bow to their parents and elders and wish them "happiness, prosperity, and longevity" and receive lucky money in red envelopes.

In chapter 6 I will discuss how Catholics can celebrate Tet within their faith tradition. Here suffice it to say that Tet embodies all the fundamental values of Vietnamese culture. It shows the Vietnamese people's gratitude to Heaven, their filial piety toward their ancestors, and their sense of national unity.

These feelings are encapsulated in the two glutinous rice cakes that are served during Tet, called *banh giay* and *banh chung*. Legend has it that King Hung Vuong the Sixth wanted to hand over the kingdom to one of his twenty-two sons. To choose the most qualified, he told them to go in search of the most tasty dish; the person whose food was judged the best would inherit the kingdom. One of the princes, Lang Lieu, whose mother had died, had no one to help, so a genie appeared to him in a dream and told him a recipe to make two cakes with glutinous rice, bean paste, and bits of pork, wrap them in banana leaves, and tie them up with bamboo strings. *Banh giay* is round, and *banh chung* is square. The king judged the cakes to be the most tasty and asked the prince about the recipe and the meaning of the shapes of the cakes. The prince told the story of how he was assisted by the genie and how *banh giay,* which is round, represents Heaven, and *banh chung,* which is square, represents Earth. The two cakes symbolize the universal harmony among Heaven, Earth, and Humanity which is, as we have seen in the previous chapter, the hallmark of Vietnamese culture.

Weddings

A Vietnamese wedding, just as those of other ethnic groups, is rich in cultural symbolism and religious meanings. Although traditional wedding customs have changed significantly, especially in the Vietnamese Diaspora, certain rituals are still faithfully observed. Of course, arranged marriages are no longer the norm, but even if the partners freely choose each other, their families are still very much involved in their engagement and wedding. Indeed, as we will see, the wedding rituals make it clear that the bride and the groom do not just marry each other, but in a real sense, each marries the other person's whole family, both the living and the dead!

Normally, the marriage ceremony has at least two parts. The first is the engagement, the main purpose of which is not so much to express the commitment of the future couple to the marriage as to secure the official consent of the bride's parents and to introduce the two families to each other. The future groom goes to the bride's home along with his parents or a distinguished elder of his family, or even a matchmaker, bringing gifts such as foods and jewelry. He is officially and formally introduced to the bride's parents and family, and the bride is formally and officially introduced to the groom's parents and family, even though both sides may already know each other well. His parents make a formal request for the consent of marriage, and negotiations about the marriage take place in which the future bride and groom do not normally take part. Most often the whole ceremony has an air of solemn play acting, and the participants themselves know it, since the decision about the marriage has already been made, but the ritual must be performed in all seriousness for the sake of propriety and tradition. The ceremony is concluded with a sumptuous dinner, the expenses of which are borne by the bride's family.

The second part is the wedding itself. On a propitious day and time, led by an elderly man, the groom's family marches in procession to the bride's home, followed by his parents, the best man and the men in the wedding party, and all the members of his extended family. They bring gifts such as betel leaves and areca nuts (which are symbols of marital love and fidelity), foods, usually a roasted pig, bottles of alcohol, and boxes of tea and sweets, all wrapped in red paper, the color of good luck.

The family is met at the door and led to the living room, where an ancestral altar has been set up. The two families line up on either side of the altar. Once again, the groom's parents make a formal request to the bride's parents for their consent to marriage, to which the latter give a rather formulaic agreement. Then the bride, who stays with the bridesmaids in a nearby room, is brought in and is formally introduced to the groom's family. The groom's mother and her mother then give her jewelry of various kinds, accompanied by tearful encouragements to be a good daughter-in-law and wife. Next, each member of the two families is introduced to the bride and groom, who are told how to address them correctly (e.g., uncle, aunt, brother, sister, etc.).

Finally, the most sacred part of the wedding ritual takes place, sealing the marriage. The bride and groom stand in front of the ancestral altar, hold several burning joss sticks in both hands, and make three deep bows to the ancestors in prayerful silence. Next, they are given a small cup of wine and they offer it to their parents as a sign of filial piety and gratitude for their gift of life and love. The ceremony concludes with each family giving gifts (usually money) to the bride and groom to help them pay for the expenses of the wedding.

After the wedding ceremony at home, Catholics go to the church for the wedding Mass, and Buddhists to the pagoda for the monk's blessing. Almost without exception the wedding is celebrated with a sit-down sumptuous banquet at a restaurant (almost never a reception only) to which not rarely a few hundred guests are invited. It is a common custom that guests give the newlyweds gifts of money rather than things, to help them defray the banquet expenses. (Americans may be pleased to know that according to Vietnamese custom, the parents of the bride do not pay for the wedding expenses; rather, it is the parents of the groom, or more often, the groom and the bride. After all, it is the bride's parents who "lose" a daughter to the groom's family!)

There are of course variations in these rituals, but the essential meaning of the wedding remains: it is a celebration of the two extended families and not simply of the couple by themselves. The ancestors are invoked, the new husband and wife are introduced to them, each of them acquiring a new set of relationships, as a new son or daughter, a new grandson or granddaughter, a new nephew or niece, as the case may be, of those who have died. In fact, each of them marries a whole new family, composed of the living and the dead. It is this (in addition to the sacrament or the ritual at the pagoda) that makes a wedding a sacred, and not simply civil and social, ceremony for the Vietnamese. These new relationships will sustain the new couple in their marriage, in good health and in sickness, in want and in plenty.

Funerals

Westerners are often puzzled by the way funerals are conducted among the Vietnamese, sometimes more sumptuously than births and weddings, especially if the deceased came from a wealthy family and had many children and grandchildren. As has been mentioned above, most Vietnamese, at least in Vietnam, do not celebrate their birthdays; rather, it is their funerals and the anniversaries of their deaths that are celebrated with elaborate rituals.

The Vietnamese, like other people, prefer to die at home rather than in the hospital, and many expatriates even plan to return to Vietnam to die there or at least to be buried among their ancestors. Even today, embalming is rarely done in Vietnam. The rituals of preparing the corpse for burial and placing it in the coffin, which in the recent past were quite elaborate, are done by members of the family, in the presence of children, who are thus exposed to the reality of death and mourning early in their lives. A photograph of the deceased is placed in front of the coffin, replacing the older wooden tablet, with the name of the deceased as well as the dates of birth and death inscribed on it. Joss sticks are lit, and visitors who come to pay their respects take them and hold them in both hands and make deep bows to the casket.

One preburial ritual that is still practiced, even in the United States, is called *le thanh phuc* (literally: the dressing ceremony). After the body is enclosed in the casket, the members of the family put on mourning clothes, made of a very low-grade white gauze (white, and not black, is the color of mourning). Often the shape of the clothes expresses the relationship the mourners have with the deceased. Another ceremony, called *le khien dien* or *le chuyen cuu,* is the announcement made to the ancestors that one of their offspring has died. Of course, in the United States, since all the preburial preparations are done by professionals and the corpse is kept at the funeral home, many of the traditional rituals have been simplified or omitted.

The next stage of the funeral is the religious celebration, Catholics at the church for the funeral Mass, Buddhists at the pagoda. Then follows the procession to the cemetery. In Vietnam this is a huge and expensive affair if the family is wealthy. Musicians with wind and string instruments and trumpets, mourners, banners, and a ten-foot painted hearse are hired for the occasion. Walking behind the hearse is the family, led by the eldest son, relatives, and friends, many of them crying loudly. At the gravesite, the family will take extreme care that the coffin is properly placed. Contrary to Western customs, the family will watch the burial, each member throwing a handful of dirt into the grave, and will not leave until the burial is completed. As has been mentioned above, the family will have a sumptuous banquet on the forty-ninth and one hundredth days after the death and also on the first anniversary. During the mourning period, members of the family wear a small black piece of material on their shirts or dresses. The mourning period lasts one year for relatives on the maternal side, three years for those on the paternal side. During this time, all festive celebrations in the family, especially weddings, must be avoided.

The greatest challenge for any ethnic group living outside of their country is how to preserve their cultural and religious customs and traditions, together with the values they embody. Chapter 6 will make a few suggestions for cultivating them. No doubt, for the younger generation of Vietnamese steeped in the American ethos some of these look quaint and old-fashioned, and the rhythm of life in the United States makes the material observance of many of them impossible. But there is no reason why the profound values they embody should not continue to inform the way of life of Vietnamese expatriates. They will be much poorer if these customs and traditions are forgotten or lost.

Chapter 4

WHO ARE VIETNAMESE AMERICANS?

LIVING BETWIXT AND BETWEEN IN THE NEW COUNTRY

Few Americans above the age of forty today would not be able to recall scenes of chaos and panic engulfing South Vietnam in the final days of April 1975. As the American ambassador Graham Martin and the last eleven Marines, bearing the American flag, were plucked by helicopters out of the American embassy in the early hours of April 30, 1975, and as hordes of frantic and frightened Southern Vietnamese, both civilian and military, stampeded to escape by air and by sea from the advancing army of Communist North Vietnam, the ten-thousand-day Vietnam conflict, the twentieth century's longest and most controversial war, came to a sudden end. Overnight South Vietnam disintegrated and vanished as a nation, and the United States, one of the world's most awesome military powers, was shamefully defeated.

Within weeks America welcomed to its soil more than 100,000 Vietnamese refugees. They were temporarily housed in various camps, the largest of which was located at the U.S. Marine Corps base in Pendleton, California, which they were allowed to leave only if sponsored by American individuals or organizations. Within a few months, however, these camps were emptied, as refugees found sponsorship, a great tribute to American generosity and the efficiency of various settlement organizations, in particular Catholic Charities.

As we will see, the first wave of Vietnamese refugees was soon joined by a succession of others, very different in many respects from their predecessors, so that the portrait of a Vietnamese refugee grew quite complex. These later refugees were scattered first in various Asian countries such as the Philippines, Thailand, Malaysia, Indonesia, and Hong Kong. Many of them were eventually allowed to settle in the United States, while others chose to migrate to Canada, Australia, and some European countries. A few were even forced to repatriate. It is estimated that currently there are 3 million Vietnamese expatriates in 37 countries.

Countless books and articles have analyzed the political and military aspects of the Vietnam War and its aftermath, and it does not appear likely that the river of ink will run dry any time soon as attempts are continually made to discern the motives and objectives, the successes and failures, and the moral lessons (if any) of this first television war of which apparently nothing seen on television (except the commercials) made sense. The ghost of this war continues to haunt the U.S. government and its foreign and defense policies, either as an incentive for self-redemption or as a cautionary tale for any American military adventure, be it in Yugoslavia, Afghanistan, or Iraq.

Much less is known, however, about the Vietnamese, or more precisely, Vietnamese Americans themselves who have made their home in the new country for three decades. Because of the dearth of up-to-date sociological studies of Vietnamese immigrants in the United States, this chapter can offer little more than a blurry snapshot of Vietnamese Americans in general, postponing a consideration of Vietnamese-American Catholics to the following chapter. We first take a brief look at the history of Vietnamese immigration to the United States. Next we examine the challenges facing Vietnamese Americans as they try to make their permanent home in their new country. Finally, we investigate the ways in which Vietnamese Americans can adapt to respond to these challenges.

Vietnamese in America

Before 1975 Vietnam was known to most Americans only through television as images of bloody battlefields and burning villages and pictures of bodies of American and Vietnamese soldiers were brought daily into their living rooms. Before that year, there were only 18,000 Vietnamese living in America, mostly students and the families of businessmen and diplomats.[1] Their numbers shot up exponentially after the fall of South Vietnam. After three decades since their settlement on these shores, the number of Vietnamese Americans is estimated at slightly over one million. The 2000 Census reported the Vietnamese population at 1,122,528.

Vietnamese refugees came to the United States in five successive waves. The first wave consisted of about 130,000 who arrived in the immediate aftermath of the collapse of South Vietnam in April 1975. The second was made up of ethnic Chinese, mainly of Cho Lon near Ho Chi Minh City, who were expelled by the Vietnamese government in 1978–79. The third was composed of 300,000 "boat people" who escaped Vietnam at great risk and came between 1978 and 1982 after being temporarily sheltered in refugee camps in various Asian countries. The fourth consisted of a much smaller number of people who were reunited with their families through various

---

1. See Ruben Rumbaut, "Vietnamese, Laotian, and Cambodian Americans," in *Asian Americans: Contemporary Issues and Trends,* ed. Pyong Gap Min (Thousand Oaks, CA: Sage, 1995), 232–70.

official programs sponsored by the United States, such as the Orderly Departure Program and Humanitarian Operations, between 1983 and 1989. The fifth was made up of those who came after March 14, 1989.[2] A small number of Vietnamese still continue to come to the United States as they are sponsored by family members, now citizens of the United States, and as the normalization of political relations between the two countries permits Vietnamese to travel to America as tourists and students.

In terms of education and professional training, the Vietnamese of the first wave were noticeably superior to those of the four later groups, which consisted mostly of students, small business owners, farmers, fishermen, craftsmen, unskilled laborers, young men fleeing the military draft for the war against Cambodia, and children sent to America by their parents to have a better life. These people had much lower levels of education, fewer job skills, and practically no knowledge of English, and therefore experienced much more difficulty in adjusting to the new environment.[3]

In terms of religious affiliation, Vietnamese refugees and immigrants represent the whole spectrum of religious traditions in Vietnam, from the indigenous religion often called animism, to the three ancient imported religions (Buddhism, Confucianism, and Taoism), to the native religions of Caodaism and Hoa Hao Buddhism, and of course to Christianity (Catholic and Protestant). Though Catholic

---

2. See James M. Freeman, *Changing Identities: Vietnamese Americans 1975–1995* (Boston: Allyn and Bacon, 1995), 29–41.
3. See Darrel Montero, *Vietnamese Americans: Patterns of Resettlement in the United States* (Boulder, CO: Westview, 1979); Nathan Caplan, John K. Whitmore, and Marcella H. Choy, *The Boat People and Achievement in America: A Study of Family Life, Hard Work, and Cultural Values* (Ann Arbor: University of Michigan Press, 1989); and Paul James Rutledge, *The Vietnamese Experience in America* (Bloomington and Indianapolis: University of Indiana Press, 1992).

Christians, as will be shown in the following chapter, make up only 8 percent of the total population in Vietnam, in the United States they represent 30 percent of Vietnamese Americans. The reason for this high proportion in America is that many Vietnamese Americans are Catholics who had fled North Vietnam to the South in 1954 to escape communism. Having had firsthand experiences of the evils of communism, they had much greater incentives to emigrate in 1975.

Like most other recently arrived ethnic groups, the Vietnamese tend to settle close to each other. California has the largest number of Vietnamese (Orange County, which has a city named Little Saigon, and San Jose), followed by Texas (Houston, Dallas/Fort Worth, and Port Arthur), Louisiana (New Orleans), Virginia, and Washington, D.C.

As a whole, Vietnamese Americans, who along with other Asian groups are often called a "model minority" or even "America's trophy population," have done well in the new country, as evidenced by their economic and professional success and the high achievements of their children at all levels of education.[4] Their economic success, all the more remarkable for such a short span of time, is accounted for not only by their Puritan-like ethics of hard work and thrift but also by their practice of providing financial assistance to family members. Their children's academic achievements may be attributed to their Confucian appreciation for education, for which parents are willing to make huge sacrifices. A Vietnamese proverb says: *Con hon cha la nha co phuc*

---

4. On the educational achievements of Vietnamese Americans, see Nathan Caplan, Marcella H. Choy, and John K. Whitmore, *Children of the Boat People: A Study of Educational Success* (Ann Arbor: Michigan University Press, 1991), and Freeman, *Changing Identities,* 69–86. Freeman writes: "The academic achievements of Vietnamese schoolchildren in America are almost legendary: valedictorians of high schools and colleges, a Rhodes scholar, winners of science competitions, high grade point averages, high scores on the Scholastic Aptitude [now Assessment] Test" (69).

(A family is blessed when the children are doing better than their parents). A stroll through Vietnamese towns such as Little Saigon in Orange County, California, with row upon row of buildings housing restaurants, small businesses, and professional services of all kinds, will give a vivid sense of the vibrancy of Vietnamese-American communities.

Yet beneath this layer of admirable achievements lie pockets of poverty, especially among the later immigrants who do not speak English well and have no marketable skills, and worrisome social and psychological problems. Furthermore, first-generation Vietnamese Americans, who have coped more or less successfully with the demands of living in a new society and culture, are now growing older and are facing a new set of challenges that go beyond physical and economic survival. On the other hand, second- and third-generation Vietnamese Americans are facing problems and questions of their own concerning their self-identity and cultural roots.

It has been said facetiously—but not without a grain of truth—that first-generation Vietnamese Americans are concerned about how to be American *Vietnamese* and describe themselves primarily as Vietnamese; second-generation Vietnamese Americans strive to be Vietnamese *American* and see themselves primarily as Americans; and third-generation Vietnamese Americans recognize that they are *both* American *and* Vietnamese and are deeply ambivalent about their primary identity. Needless to say, all three kinds of Vietnamese Americans have their own problems and challenges, a fact that it is wise to remember as we seek to understand them.

Challenges to Vietnamese Americans

The challenges facing Vietnamese Americans, while overlapping to a certain extent, are distinct for each generation. As with any other group of immigrants and refugees, first-generation Vietnamese Americans, less familiar with the English language and American cultural customs, and more attached to those of their homeland, are more concerned with economic survival than with cultural issues. For them, the most pressing concerns are finding shelter and work, learning to speak the new language as best they can, knowing that they will never master it, and adjusting to the new environment despite the barriers of poverty, prejudice, discrimination, and minority status. Most often they settle in Vietnamese enclaves, consort almost exclusively with other Vietnamese, speak Vietnamese among themselves, dress in their native clothing (women in *ao dai* on formal occasions), shop at Vietnamese stores, eat their own Vietnamese foods, worship at Vietnamese churches or pagodas, celebrate Vietnamese feasts and festivals (in particular, Tet), observe the Vietnamese customs (especially at weddings and funerals), and generally behave as if they were still living in their old country. Their overwhelming goal is to have their children well educated and to help them achieve upward mobility in American society.

By contrast, for those of the second and third generations, who often speak English fluently and broken or no Vietnamese at all, and for whom all things Vietnamese appear quaint, the challenge is not so much how to fit into American culture and society (they have grown up in America) but how to define themselves racially, ethnically, and culturally. This need to define oneself in racial, ethnic, and cultural terms, it may be noted, is unique to more recent non-European immigrants, since their skin color and physical features do not identify them at first sight as Americans, no matter how long they have lived in the United States or how well they have blended into its cultural landscape. This need to find one's racial, ethnic, and cultural roots is being strongly encouraged by the ethos of multiculturalism, which has challenged if not replaced the older ideal of the melting pot. In this context culture is experienced less as an integrated and integrative, homogeneous, well-defined whole, as we have seen in the previous chapter, and more as a historically evolving and conflicted social reality.

In what follows I highlight some of the areas in which Vietnamese and American cultural values and customs are likely to collide, and therefore pose difficult challenges to Vietnamese Americans as they live betwixt and between the two cultures and attempt to acculturate to their new environment.

Family Challenges

It comes as no surprise that the greatest challenges and the most common source of conflict arise in the family, since, as we saw in the previous chapter, the family is where the Vietnamese cultural and religious values are most deeply embodied and where cultural differences between Vietnam and America are most pronounced. The Vietnamese family is by and large patriarchal (the supreme authority residing in the father), androcentric (favoring the male), extended (two or three generations living under the same roof and with intimate ties with one's uncles, aunts, and cousins), privileging the family's common good (parents making sacrifices for their children, the children obeying and respecting their elders, willingness to forego one's personal happiness for the sake of the group), governed by tradition and rule (especially the duties of filial piety and propriety), and self-interested (most concerned about the welfare of the family's members and generally opposed to intermarriage).

By contrast, American society and culture, and in particular the American family, are perceived, fairly or not, as undermining the values associated with the Vietnamese family. Most troubling to the Vietnamese is American individualism, with its almost absolute claims to autonomy (e.g., moving out of the house before marriage and keeping one's earnings rather than contributing to the family's finances), freedom (often seen as lack of self-discipline and permissiveness, especially in sexual matters), the pursuit of personal self-fulfillment (viewed as selfishness and eagerness for immediate self-gratification, rather than willingness to sacrifice oneself for the common good and the reputation of the family), and individual self-determination (regarded as lack of gratitude and deference to the parents rather than obeying their wishes in matters of career and marriage). Vietnamese Americans tend to see teenage pregnancy, abortion, divorce, homosexuality, and sexual crime in America as the result of the American family system and its underlying values.

Of course conflicts between parents and children, between traditional (Confucian) values and modern (Western) ideals, and between old and new generations are not a novelty for the Vietnamese. Acrimonious debates about these differences were very much in the air in Vietnam in the 1930s and since then, traditional Vietnamese society has suffered significant erosions not only because of the impact of Western ideas but also because of the destructive effects of the war on family arrangements. Nevertheless, the current cultural conflict about the family among Vietnamese Americans is different given the absence of societal and cultural structures supporting the traditional values and the overwhelming pressure to conform to the new way of life in America. Consequently, Vietnamese families often feel isolated and alienated, which makes conflicts between parents and children, and between husband and wife, much more intense and less amenable to resolution.

Family crises in Vietnamese-American families usually focus on two issues: the role of women and the duties of children. First-generation Vietnamese-American men, accustomed to male-dominated ways of life, often experience confusion and threat as their wives, who must work to make ends meet and who usually acculturate faster, become more financially independent and assertive. Having lost everything that gave them a strong sense of security such as material possessions, friends, relatives, career, social status, and country, and now with their authority diminished, their masculinity challenged, and their self-identity in tatters, Vietnamese men fall easy prey to alcoholism and depression as well as to becoming child and spouse abusers.

The parent-child relationship, especially between father and daughter, is also subject to a good deal of stress. Vietnamese parents are very protective of their daughters, particularly in matters of dating and spouse selection. For girls dating is strongly discouraged until after college, and teenage pregnancies have so far been relatively rare. Though Asian-American women seem to select spouses outside their own ethnic group at a higher rate than men, their marriage to non-Vietnamese (especially to blacks) is often frowned upon, partly due to racism and partly due to the perception, common during the Vietnam War, that only Vietnamese girls of doubtful morality would marry an American. As for boys, the pressure is to excel academically and they are pushed very hard by their parents to study for lucrative careers such as medicine, law, and engineering rather than majoring in the humanities such as literature and religious studies. In order to be able to send their children to the best schools, parents often have to work long hours, especially if they own small businesses, and as a result, have little contact with their children.

Needless to say, in both husband-wife and parent-child relationships, Vietnamese Americans, especially of the first generation, run a high risk of incurring psychological disorders, besides resorting to physical violence, as mentioned above. Adolescents fall victim to drugs, and there have been criminal gangs that recruit maladjusted youths to rob and extort their fellow Vietnamese. Vietnamese girls, exposed to the American idea of gender equality, chafe at parental and male control. It is also a fact that educational performance declines and divorce rates rise with the second and third generations. In spite of severe psychological problems in the family, Vietnamese Americans are reluctant to seek professional counseling because they traditionally avoid discussing personal problems with strangers and because mental illness is regarded as a stigma.

Social Challenges

As a "model minority," Vietnamese Americans have been praised for their work ethic, frugality, self-reliance, and initiative. Their economic success, professional achievements, and academic excellence have been celebrated by the media. Never before in American history, it is reported, has a group of refugees succeeded so well so fast. But this "model minority" status, while certainly well deserved, can be a curse in disguise. It hides the fact that among successful Vietnamese Americans, there are others (in particular, the "boat people," who made up roughly 40 percent of Vietnamese refugees in the 1980s, and former political prisoners) who have had a much tougher time making it economically and adjusting to the new environment. Because of the lack of professional skills and a sufficient knowledge of English, these individuals (many of them women) are employed by Vietnamese businesses in menial jobs, serve around the clock in restaurants as waiters and waitresses, frequently at less than the minimum wage, are without medical or unemployment insurance, or work long hours at home for the garment industry. They dare not complain or protest for fear of being dismissed.

Furthermore, socially, two segments of the Vietnamese-American population currently deserve special attention. The first group is the elderly, whose numbers are on the rise.

Contrary to the American custom of placing older parents (however reluctantly) in retirement homes, the Vietnamese consider it a sin of filial impiety to do so. The unintended but sad result is that the elderly are kept at home, lonely and without adequate care, and without healthy contacts with the outside world, while their children are at work and their grandchildren are at school.

The second group is youth. Vietnamese criminal gangs rob stores and extort payments from merchants, especially in Little Saigon, and break into the houses of affluent Vietnamese to steal valuables. While these gangs, whose criminal activities have been sensationalized by the American popular media, are wholly unrepresentative of the overwhelming majority of Vietnamese youth, there is no doubt that Vietnamese youth are currently a group most at risk. More than any other Vietnamese-American cohort, Vietnamese youth truly live betwixt and between two cultures, belonging to neither fully.

The challenges facing Vietnamese youth (i.e., second-generation Vietnamese Americans) are many, diverse, and over-whelming. At home, they are not understood by their parents (sometimes literally, since they often do not speak Vietnamese well); they are bound by a cultural and moral code they perceive to be strange and unreasonable. At school, they are pressured to succeed well to please their parents but are taunted by their classmates. They are also handicapped academically because though born and raised in this country, they may not have a good command of English since it is not the language spoken at home. Socially, they feel somehow different because of their racial and ethnic background. At times they are victims of racial discrimination. When they try to fit in with the Anglo majority, they are mocked by other Vietnamese as "bananas," or "yellow on the outside but white on the inside." Yet, among the Anglos who may befriend them, they are still segregated as an ethnic group. Morally, they are highly susceptible to the enticements, powerfully purveyed by the media, of individualism, consumerism, materialism, sexual permissiveness, and secularism, things that run counter to the values they are taught at home. Religiously, they still go to church or the pagoda with their parents, but the worship service they attend is totally incomprehensible to them. Culturally, their identity is assaulted by ambivalence and uncertainty. Externally, they behave like Americans, but deep down they feel they do not (as yet) belong to America: Anglos still ask them where they come from—and when they are going home. And yet, they know nothing about Vietnamese history, geography, language, literature, and culture, about which they hear constantly. All in all, Vietnamese-American youth dwell at the margins of two cultures, attracted to both but repelled by both, not sufficiently American for the one and not sufficiently Vietnamese for the other. And yet, the future of the American-Vietnamese community is vested in them, and the burden is not an easy one to bear.

Finally, Vietnamese-Americans have been branded by widespread social misconceptions—that a high percentage of them are on welfare, that they have received special treatment from the government in the form of interest-free loans to buy cars and houses, that they take jobs away from other minority groups, and that their youth are prone to violence. While studies have shown that none of these accusations is true, it is a challenge to dispel these oft-repeated pieces of folklore in the society at large.

Political Challenges

Most Americans are immigrants or descendants of immigrants; they know firsthand or through family stories something of the hardships that befall immigrants. But there is an important difference between them and Vietnamese Americans: most of the latter were not immigrants but *refugees.* Immigrants voluntarily leave their countries of origin, often for economic reasons. Refugees, by contrast, are forced to flee their homelands, often suddenly and at great risk of life and limb, because of political, ethnic, or religious persecution. In addition to the usual difficulties connected with the process of adjustment to the new environment, there are much deeper psychological pains stemming from the loss of one's past and the uncertainty about one's future. The sense of security provided by one's past accomplishments vanishes, and the sense of purpose undergirded by control over one's future is also taken away. Consequently, many older Vietnamese Americans, living betwixt and between, are consumed by nostalgia for their past and depression about their future.

Keeping this distinction between immigrant and refugee in mind will be helpful in understanding the political stance of many Vietnamese Americans. As refugees from communism, they look upon America as the land of freedom. On the other hand, having suffered grievously from the despotic and corrupt regimes of their homeland, they are not familiar with the democratic process and therefore distrust government. This anomalous situation partially accounts for the contradictory fact that while they champion the freedoms guaranteed by the American Constitution, they will go to any length to suppress any expression of opinion or speech and any action (e.g., doing business) in favor of the Socialist Republic of Vietnam. Many were opposed to the normalization of political relations between the United States and Vietnam. A few still nurture the illusion of a regime change in Vietnam, even through military action. Most would strongly object to the public display of the flag of the Socialist Republic of Vietnam and continue to fly that of the former Republic of Vietnam (yellow background with three horizontal red stripes). For many Vietnamese Americans, *cong san* (communist) is a term of political abuse.

This rabid anticommunist stance among Vietnamese Americans is understandable if one recalls that they had to flee communism and that many of them have personally suffered at the hands of the Communists or had relatives killed by them. Furthermore, as has been mentioned above, a large percentage of Vietnamese Americans are Catholic and have been traditionally opposed to communism. Many Vietnamese Catholics agitate against religious restrictions in Vietnam and demand the restitution of Church properties confiscated by the government since 1975.

Like many other Asian groups, Vietnamese Americans are averse to taking part in politics by running for public office, partly because they have not yet developed a strong sense of public service, putting the welfare of their family above that of the larger community, partly because they view politics as less rewarding than business and less prestigious than education. In terms of electoral politics, a majority of older Vietnamese Americans favor the Republican Party, because it is perceived as tough on communism and favorable to business, though this appears not to be the case with Vietnamese-American college students.

Whatever their political stance toward the Socialist Republic of Vietnam, however, Vietnamese Americans have been very generous in giving financial assistance to their people back home, especially in times of personal tragedy and natural disaster. It is estimated that in 2001 Vietnamese expatriates sent home $2 billion. They practice what a Vietnamese proverb says: *La lanh dum la rach* (Whole leaves must cover torn ones). Though not too attentive to American politics, Vietnamese Americans, thanks to a plethora of print, radio, television, and computer media, follow important events in Vietnam very closely and rally to the assistance of their people, irrespective of their political opinions and choices.

Different Customs, Different Practices

Americans may find a few Vietnamese customs and practices unusual and even disconcerting. While these customs and practices may no longer be widespread among second-generation Vietnamese Americans, knowledge of them may prevent misunderstanding.

1. In addressing the Vietnamese, it is advisable to use their titles (e.g., Mr., Mrs., Miss, Dr., Professor, etc.). The Vietnamese do not call their American superiors or priests by their first names, even if they are friends. Indeed, doing so may indicate improper relationships.

2. The Vietnamese, especially women, greet their superiors and priests by bowing, rarely by shaking hands. Needless to say, gestures that are common among Americans such as kissing a cheek, placing a hand on another person's shoulder, patting the head, and hugging (especially Vietnamese women) are not proper.

3. The Vietnamese avoid conflict, especially with their superiors. If asked to do something that they find burdensome, they will not say "no" for fear of disrespect. They will say "yes," but "yes" does not always mean agreement, only that the request has been acknowledged. They tend not to look into the eyes of their superiors when talking to them, out of respect and not deviousness.

4. After doing something wrong, the Vietnamese tend to smile when reprimanded by their superiors. This does not mean that they do not take the mistake and the reprimand seriously but indicates embarrassment. Avoid at all costs a loud voice in reprimanding, especially with an older person.

5. Never sit on a desk or put your feet on the desk in the presence of older Vietnamese. It is perceived as arrogance, not casualness.

6. Never call an older Vietnamese by wagging a finger, which is a sign of impoliteness. Use the whole hand with the palm turned down.

7. It is proper to give money as a gift, especially at weddings. If gifts are given, give them in pairs.

8. The Vietnamese do not "go dutch" at restaurants. It is expected that the superior will pay the whole bill. If not, it is better to take turns.

9. The Vietnamese prefer to make their wishes known indirectly. Straight talk suggests aggressiveness.

10. The Vietnamese consider it immodest to speak of their accomplishments, even in interviews for jobs. To know their real background, ask explicit questions about their talents and achievements.

Responding to the Challenges: Toward a Vietnamese-American Culture

In the last three decades Vietnamese Americans have adopted different strategies to meet these multiple challenges. Having come to the United States not of their own free will, some, perhaps most, of the first generation, have resisted the cultural changes, making only the minimum adaptation necessary to survive economically and to ensure a bright future for their children. Lacking the necessary knowledge of English and unfamiliar with the new ways of life, they feel that American culture undermines their traditional values and attempt to preserve the Vietnamese way of life as much as possible, often in separate enclaves or cultural ghettos. They look back with nostalgia to the old days when they were "somebody" and look forward with anticipation to an eventual return to their homeland to spend the final days of their lives.

Others, perhaps most of the second generation, have appropriated all the features of American culture, good and bad, ending up not knowing even the language of their parents and thinking and acting like Americans, though they are never fully accepted because of the color of their skin. The high price for their complete acculturation and professional success is a loss of cultural identity, a subconscious shame of their ethnic roots, and a nagging question about what makes them who they really are.

A very small group, mainly youth, have refused the American way of life altogether, either because they have severe psychological problems and are therefore incapable of adjustment or because they are marginalized by American society, especially its educational system. Without job skills and community support, they try to subvert the system through violence and crime.

Finally, there are those who, aware of the positive and negative features of both Vietnamese and American cultures, attempt to synthesize a new Vietnamese-American culture, not only for themselves in the United States but also as a model to guide the rebuilding of Vietnam. The goal is to eliminate the defects and preserve the most valuable elements of the traditional Vietnamese way of life and to enhance these positive aspects with the best that American culture can offer.

Negative elements in Vietnamese culture include the following:

- an endemic spirit of division and mutual opposition which sets up rivalry among the people of the north, the center, and the south of Vietnam; among political parties; among religions (in particular, between Buddhism and Catholicism); and among community groups;
- little concern for the common good: top priority is given to the well-being of one's family, and at best of one's clan; consequently, there is no strong sense of nationhood or patriotism

- no conception of power and authority as public service; instead, positions of power are used to enrich oneself or one's family or to enhance one's fame and reputation
- lack of a genuine democracy: those in power seek to perpetuate their domination through dictatorship and family rule, and the people are indifferent to the political process
- overemphasis on formalities and rituals: little attention is given to substantive issues when action is called for
- patriarchal and androcentric family system: abuse of the authority of the father and suppression of the rights of women
- excessive emphasis on conformity to tradition in moral education: little importance attached to the formation of conscience and personal responsibility
- education as rote learning and as technical preparation for lucrative jobs: scarce appreciation of education as formation of the mind and soul and training for critical thinking through the liberal arts
- excessive concern for "feelings" and relationships rather than following objective criteria in judging truth and moral goodness
- overemphasis on harmony as the goal in itself rather than attempting to resolve conflict through reasonable means

Needless to say, there are elements in American culture that can be harnessed to correct these deficiencies of the Vietnamese culture. In particular, the following are important:

- recognition of the equality of all human beings
- respect for the basic freedoms and human rights

- maintenance of the rule of law
- establishment of democratic institutions
- separation of church and state
- promotion of a rightful place of religion in public life
- concern for the common good
- collaboration in spite of political differences
- voluntarism
- patriotism
- unity amid racial, ethnic, cultural, and religious pluralism
- solidarity with the poor
- stress on personal responsibility
- education as a total formation of the human person

A Vietnamese-American culture will appropriate these positive aspects of American culture and combine them with the values stressed by Vietnamese culture that we discussed in chapter 2. In this way, the excesses of the American way of life (such as individualism, consumerism, and materialism) can be tempered and Vietnamese culture can be greatly enriched. Vietnamese Americans are challenged to make this hybrid culture a reality. Living betwixt and between two cultures, though the result of a national tragedy, is in hindsight a providential blessing for Vietnam, since the possibility has now arisen, for the first time in its history, to create, through the agency of Vietnamese Americans, a culture that is a marriage of the best elements of East and West, a proof that Rudyard Kipling's oft-quoted dictum "Oh, East is East, and West is West, and never the twain shall meet" is vastly wrong unless it is accompanied by the next verse: "But there is neither East nor West, border, nor breed, nor birth."

Chapter 5

WHO ARE VIETNAMESE CATHOLICS?

A BRIEF HISTORY OF VIETNAMESE CHRISTIANITY

Of the slightly over one million Vietnamese in America in the year 2000, 30 percent were Catholic, a significantly higher percentage than in Vietnam, where they made up 6 percent of the total population of 80 million. But numbers alone do not present the true picture of Catholic Vietnamese Americans. To understand them one needs to know the kind of Christianity that has shaped and nurtured them. This chapter offers a brief historical survey of Catholic Christianity in Vietnam, with the focus on the present situation.

The Early Years of Vietnamese Christianity

Christianity appears to have entered Vietnam for the first time in the third decade of the sixteenth century. According to the Vietnamese Imperial Historical Records *(Kham Dinh Viet Su Thong Giam Cuong Muc)* published in 1884, there was, in 1533, under the reign of King Le Trang Ton, a rescript proscribing the *Da-to ta dao* (false Christian religion). This new religion is said to have been preached by a certain I-Ni-Khu (Ignatius) in two villages (Ninh Cuong and Tra Lu) in the province of Nam Dinh, North Vietnam. Between 1550 and 1615, Dominican missionaries from the Philippines and Malacca came to Vietnam, but their activities left no noticeable traces.

Christian mission was consolidated with the arrival from Macao of Jesuit priests Francesco Buzomi and Diego Carvalho and three lay brothers at Cua Han, Quang Nam, in 1615. From 1615 to 1659, the bulk of missionary work was carried out by the Jesuits (mostly Portuguese) of whom the most famous was the French Alexandre de Rhodes (1593–1660).

De Rhodes arrived in Central Vietnam in December 1624, and after a few months of language study, he was sent with Pêro Marquez to the north (Tonkin), arriving there on March 19, 1627. After almost four highly successful years, he was expelled from the country, went back to Macao in 1630, remained there for ten years, and in 1640 returned to Central Vietnam. For five years, during which he was expelled four times, de Rhodes conducted clandestine missionary activities. On July 3, 1645, de Rhodes was expelled from Vietnam for good.

De Rhodes's accomplishments were extraordinary. Not only did he succeed in bringing about a huge number of conversions (estimated at ten thousand), he also produced three long-lasting achievements. First, he set up an organization of lay catechists, of whom two were later martyred, to assist him in the evangelizing work and to guide the church during the missionaries' absence. Second, after 1645, he went to Rome to lobby for the establishment of a hierarchy in Vietnam. As a result of his tenacious efforts in the face of fierce opposition by the Portuguese crown, in 1658 Pope Alexander VII appointed François Pallu bishop of Tonkin and Pierre Lambert de la Motte bishop of Cochinchina. Third, he was the leading contributor to the modern Vietnamese script, now known as the national script, using the Roman alphabet and diacritical marks to distinguish the various tones of the Vietnamese language, and was the author of a dictionary and a catechism in Vietnamese.

By the middle of the seventeenth century the Church in Vietnam was growing by leaps and bounds. De Rhodes reported (perhaps with a bit of exaggeration) that in 1650 there were 300,000 Catholics in the North, with a yearly increase of at least 15,000.

The Church Steeped in Blood

Missionary work in the next two centuries, though highly successful, met with grave difficulties. Some of these stemmed from the political situation of the country at the time. When Christianity first arrived in Vietnam, the reigning dynasty was the Hau Le, or Later Le, dynasty (so named to distinguish it from the Tien Le, Earlier Le, dynasty of 980–1009). The Later Le dynasty was inaugurated in 1428 by Le Loi, who assumed the name of Le Thai To after liberating the country from the Ming dynasty. It officially ended in 1788 with its last king Le Chieu Thong, but already in 1527, power had been wrested from it by the Mac dynasty, which ruled from 1527 to 1592.

In 1532 two clans, the Trinh and the Nguyen, rose up to defend the Later Le dynasty against the Mac dynasty. But the Le kings were little more than puppets and real power was in the hands of the Trinh and Nguyen. Soon rivalries divided the two clans, the former ruling over the North and the latter over the South (which at the time included only three central provinces—Quang Binh, Thuan Hoa, and Quang Nam). Military conflicts between the two families erupted in 1627, the very year de Rhodes went to the north, and lasted off and on for forty-five years. They waged seven wars until 1672, without decisive victory for either side. The country was then divided into two parts, with the River Giang as the dividing line, until it was reunified in 1802 by King Gia Long of the Nguyen clan, who named the country *Vietnam*.

The rivalry between the North and the South greatly complicated the work of missionaries as each side, especially the Trinh clan, suspected them of being spies for the other and, when convenient, used them as mediators to obtain merchandise and military wares from their countrymen, especially the Portuguese. Though the early missionaries never collaborated with colonial powers, the religion they preached was associated by the Vietnamese, wrongly but perhaps inevitably, with their imperialistic countries.

The second source of severe problems for the mission in Vietnam was the *padroado* system, initiated in 1494 by Pope Alexander VI, whereby it was agreed that the lands discovered by Portugal in Asia and Africa would belong to the Portuguese crown and that no missionary could enter them without its prior permission. At the time, the Church of Tonkin belonged to the diocese of Macao in China and the Church of Cochinchina to the diocese of Malacca in Malaysia, both located in Portuguese colonies. After de Rhodes succeeded in having French bishops appointed to the two Vietnamese dioceses and having them placed as "apostolic vicars" under the authority of the *Congregatio de Propaganda Fide* (founded in 1622 by Pope Gregory XV), a strain was created between the earlier missionaries, mostly Spanish and Portuguese Jesuits and Dominicans under the Portuguese authority, and the later missionaries who were mostly French and belonged to the *Missions Étrangères de Paris,* a society recently founded by Bishop Pallu. The jurisdictional dispute between these two groups did much harm to the missionary enterprise.

The third source of problems was what has been referred to as the Chinese Rites Controversy. This controversy began in China in the early seventeenth century in the course of which the Dominicans, the Franciscans, and the members of the Paris Foreign Missions succeeded in having the practice of offering sacrifices to Confucius and the ancestors, which the Jesuits allowed, condemned as superstition. In 1710, Pope Clement XI ratified the Holy Office's 1704 decree condemning these practices and in 1715, enjoined an oath of obedience on all missionaries to Asia. Pope Benedict XIV renewed the condemnation, insisting on the absolute rejection of the Chinese rites in his bull *Ex quo singulari* (1742).

The Chinese Rites Controversy, of course, had repercussions for Vietnam. Bishop Alexander (d. 1738) excommunicated Charles de Flory, superior of the French missionaries in South Vietnam, for allowing these rites. In 1739, Pope Clement XIII sent Bishop Achards de la Baume to Vietnam to bring about harmony in this matter. However, in 1939, *Propaganda Fide* issued, with Pope Pius XII's approval, the instruction *Plane compertum est,* permitting the veneration of ancestors insofar as it is a "civil and political act." This policy was not implemented in Vietnam until 1964. In the meantime, conversion to Christianity was much hindered by the fact that it was perceived as a religion that forbids carrying out the sacred duties of filial piety.

The last and most severe challenge to the infant Church was the numerous persecutions by various Vietnamese rulers. It is estimated that 30,000 Catholics were killed under the rule of the Trinh clan in the North and under the rule of the Nguyen clan and the Tay Son family in the South during the seventeenth and eighteenth centuries; that 40,000 were killed under the reign of 3 emperors of the Nguyen dynasty—Minh Mang (1820–40), Thieu Tri (1841–47), and Tu Duc (1848–83); and that 60,000 were killed by the Van Than movement (1864–85). Of these 130,000 killed for the faith, there were 8 bishops, more than 200 priests, 340 catechists, and 270 members of the Lovers of the Cross Society, a

Vietnamese female religious congregation founded by Bishop Pierre Lambert de La Motte. In 1988, Pope John Paul II canonized 117 of these martyrs, of whom 96 were Vietnamese (one of them was a woman, Le Thi Thanh).

On the Way to Maturity

In spite of these severe difficulties the Church expanded rapidly. In 1802, there were only 3 dioceses, with 320,000 faithful. In 1889, there were 8 dioceses, with 613,435 faithful. In 1933, the first Vietnamese bishop, Nguyen Ba Tong, was consecrated. In 1934, the first Indochinese council was held in Hanoi, with 19 bishops, 5 major religious superiors, and 21 priests participating. The council issued 426 statutes governing pastoral ministry in Indochina.

Unfortunately, no sooner had the Church begun to organize then the country was engulfed in the independence war against France. The 1954 Geneva Accords divided Vietnam into two parts, the North under the communist regime and the South under a democratic and pro-Western government. As a result of the partitioning, 860,000 Vietnamese, of whom 650,000 were Catholic, fled the North, thereby decimating the Church in the North and dramatically swelling the Catholic population of the South. After this exodus, in the 10 northern dioceses, there were 7 bishops and 327 priests left to serve some 831,500 Catholics. By contrast, in the South, according to the statistics provided by the *Propaganda Fide,* there were in 1957 1.1 million Catholics: 67,854 catechumens, 254 seminarians, 1,672 catechists, and 1,264 priests.

To commemorate the three hundredth anniversary of the establishment of the first two dioceses in Vietnam (1659–1959) and to mark the growth into maturity of the Church, a national Marian Congress was celebrated in Saigon on

February 17, 1959, under the presidency of Cardinal Gregorio Agagianian, prefect of the *Propaganda Fide.*

On December 8, 1960, with the constitution *Venerabilium nostrorum* issued on the 24th of the previous month, Pope John XXIII established the Vietnamese hierarchy, dividing the Church into three ecclesiastical provinces (Hanoi, Hue, and Saigon) with twenty ordinaries, and no longer just apostolic vicars. Thus, after four hundred years of mission, the Vietnamese Catholic Church became a full-fledged Church with its own hierarchy.

The Church in the North since 1954

Cut off from the Church in the South and the Church of Rome for almost twenty-one years (1954–75), persecuted by the communist government, devastated by the departure of large numbers of clergy and laity in 1954, the Church in the North barely survived. With its educational and social institutions confiscated by the government and its clergy practically under house arrest, the Church limited its activities to sacramental celebrations and pious devotions. It did not benefit from the great reforms instituted by Vatican II (1962–65).

In the 1990s the government adopted a more open policy toward the Church. It allowed one seminary to function in the archdiocese of Hanoi and one for the dioceses of Vinh and Thanh Hoa. In 1994 the government permitted the transfer of Bishop Nguyen Son Lam, formerly bishop of Da Lat (in the South), to the diocese of Thanh Hoa that had been *sede vacante* since 1990.

The Church in the South until 1975

Compared with the Church in the North, the Church in the South was in a far more favorable situation. Not only did it benefit from the massive influx of Catholics in 1954, it also enjoyed twenty years of freedom (1955–75) that fortunately coincided with a period of extensive renewal in the Catholic Church. The Church in the South was making rapid gains: in 1959, it had 1,226,310 Catholics: 1,342 native priests, 715 brothers, and 3,776 sisters. In addition, it exercised an extensive influence on the society at large through its numerous first-rate educational, health care, and social institutions. A Catholic university was founded in 1957 in Da Lat, and a Pontifical Theological Faculty named Pius X was established in 1958 in the same city. Other universities such as Minh Duc, Thanh Nhan, Regina Mundi, and Regina Pacis soon followed.

The Church under the Socialist Regime

Communist North Vietnam conquered the South in 1975 and when the country was reunified the following year, the Catholic Church, like all religious organizations, faced a severe challenge. All its educational and social institutions were confiscated and almost all its religious organizations were disbanded, from the committees of the Vietnamese Episcopal Conference to parish councils. Some two hundred priest-chaplains were sent to reeducation centers. Archbishop Nguyen Van Thuan, who had been appointed coadjutor with rights of succession to the archdiocese of Saigon (Ho Chi Minh City) in 1975, was imprisoned and then placed under house arrest for thirteen years, until he was expelled in 1991. Several priests and religious were falsely accused of treason, tried, and sent to prison.

In November 1983 a National Meeting of Vietnamese Catholics for the Building Up and Defense of the Country and of Peace was held in Hanoi, with some five hundred Catholics in attendance. The meeting founded an organization named *Uy Ban Doan Ket Cong Giao Yeu Nuoc* (Committee for the Unification of Nationalist Vietnamese

Catholics), with seventy-four members, among whom there was a handful of so-called state priests *(linh muc quoc doanh)*. It described itself not as a religious entity but as a member organization of the National Front of Vietnam, governed by the constitution and laws of the Socialist Republic of Vietnam. It was heavily criticized as a front to establish a Vietnamese national or patriotic church, in the Chinese model. Had the committee such an intention, which its organizers publicly disavowed, it was never realized, and its subsequent impact on the Church was minimal.

Though religious freedom is recognized in the national constitution, and though regular sacramental celebrations were allowed, special permission was required for religious activities involving a large crowd of participants. The government also restricted the number of priestly ordinations and interfered with the appointment of bishops. For example, Archbishop Nguyen Van Thuan (who later went to Rome and was made a cardinal) was prevented from succeeding Archbishop Nguyen Van Binh in the Ho Chi Minh archdiocese. In the meantime, Bishop Huynh Cong Nghi was appointed apostolic administrator of the archdiocese but was not allowed to assume office.

Since 1988, however, the communist government has adopted a more relaxed attitude toward religious institutions. Six seminaries were allowed to reopen: in Hanoi, Vinh-Thanh, Nha Trang, Ho Chi Minh, Can Tho, and Hue. The number of seminarians grew so large that in October 1993 the Vietnamese Episcopal Conference requested the opening of two more seminaries in the dioceses of Xuan Loc and Thai Binh. Besides these official seminaries, there are several underground centers where thousands of seminarians are being trained. The lack of qualified professors is drastic, and the level of academic preparation is far from satisfactory. Recently, the government permitted a number of priests and religious to go abroad, especially to France and Rome, for higher studies. Bishops, too, are regularly permitted to do their *ad limina* visits to Rome as well as to travel abroad. There have also been frequent visits by Vatican officials, which have improved relationships between Vietnam and the Holy See significantly, as well as by representatives of the American Catholic Church.

Since the late 1980s, restrictions on the publication of religious works have been somewhat eased. Works on the Bible, theology, spirituality, liturgy, and liturgical music have appeared. Of special note are new translations of the Liturgy of the Hours and the Roman Missal. Deserving the highest praise is a modern translation of the Bible with scholarly introductions and notes, the fruit of twenty years of labor by a team of fourteen translators.

Despite external difficulties, the Vietnamese Catholic Church is vibrant and growing. Vietnam has the second largest number of Catholics in Asia, after the Philippines. In 2000, it was reported that Vietnam had 25 dioceses (10 in the ecclesiastical province of Hanoi, 6 in that of Hue, and 9 in that of Ho Chi Minh City), 1 cardinal, 33 bishops, 5,380,567 faithful, 2,133 diocesan priests, 1816 religious, 9,654 sisters, and 676 seminarians.

Protestant Christianity

To complete the picture of Vietnamese Christianity, a brief word on Protestant Christianity in Vietnam is called for here. Protestant Christianity is known in Vietnam as *Tin Lanh* (Good News). Protestantism was introduced to Vietnam under the auspices of Christian and Missionary Alliance by Robert A. Jaffrey in 1911. By 1927 it had 4,115 adherents. That same year saw the establishment of the Evangelical Church of Indochina; in 1950, its name was changed to the

Evangelical Church of Vietnam. After 1954, the church's evangelizing activities were aimed at the Vietnamese in the South and at the tribal peoples inhabiting the Central Highlands. Subsequently, numerous other Protestant denominations arrived in South Vietnam and expanded the scope of Christian activities to include social and educational projects. By 1974 the Tribes Church numbered 45,000 Christians.

By 1975, the Evangelical Church of Vietnam had 510 churches with 54,000 members, 276 Bible students at Nha Trang, and 900 laypeople theologically trained by extension courses. As the result of the communist takeover of South Vietnam in 1975, most of the Tribes churches were closed, 90 pastors were sent to reeducation camps, and 3 were executed in 1978. Despite extreme difficulties, however, Protestant churches, like the Catholic Church, are experiencing a healthy revival.

Vietnamese Catholicism: A Look into the Future

Like any other brand of Catholicism, Vietnamese Catholicism has its strengths and weaknesses. Like early Christianity, it has demonstrated its faithfulness and heroism with its many martyrs. Its spectacular growth and its vibrancy, in spite of severe challenges and persecution, past and present, prove the truth of the famous dictum that the blood of martyrs is the seed of the Church. Strongly influenced by Iberian Catholicism, Vietnamese Catholics cultivate a great devotion to Mary and the saints. Implementing Vatican II's renewal programs, the Vietnamese Catholic Church has begun emphasizing the study of the Bible, socio-political engagement, solidarity with the poor, and active involvement of the laity. Remarkable, too, is the high number of vocations to priestly and religious life.

On the other hand, Vietnamese Catholicism still needs to free itself of its overemphasis on institutional structures. Associated with this institutionalism is clericalism. There is the danger that the priesthood is being used as a ladder for social promotion. In addition, religious and theological formation remains an urgent need for both clergy and laity. Because of restrictions imposed by the government, the Vietnamese Church runs the risk of self-absorption (e.g., too much focus is placed on the building of churches) and limiting its activities to sacramental and devotional celebrations, and neglecting the social and political dimensions of its ministry. Furthermore, recently members of the clergy and religious orders (including bishops) from Vietnam have begun doing fundraising among the Catholic Diaspora communities, especially in the United States. While such activities may be justified, the lack of accountability and transparency about how the funds will be used are reasons for concern.

In terms of the impact of Vietnamese Catholicism on the wider society, one aspect of its recent history deserves highlighting, and that is its many and significant contributions to the nation's culture and political independence. These achievements must be honestly and publicly recognized in view of the fact that, unlike Buddhism, Confucianism, and Taoism which, though imported from India and China, have succeeded in shaping Vietnamese culture, Vietnamese Christianity has often been accused of being a "foreign" religion. Worse, Vietnamese Catholics have been accused—unfairly—of having collaborated with colonial powers and having done little for the cause of national independence.

Concerning of national independence, the participation of Catholics (including priests) in the early anticolonialist parties such as *Viet Nam Quang Phuc Hoi* and *Viet Nam Quoc Dan Dang* needs to be remembered. In 1945, all four Vietnamese bishops lobbied publicly for national independence. Among them, Bishop Le Huu Tu (1896–1967), stood out as the fiercest defender of national independence against French colonization. In 1946 he founded *Lien Doan Cong Giao* (the Catholic League) to fight for independence and *Viet Nam Cong Giao Cuu Quoc (*Vietnamese Catholics to Save the Country) to engage Catholics in political and military service. In fact, Ho Chi Minh made him supreme counselor of the state, and it was in this capacity that the bishop protested against Ho Chi Minh after the latter signed a treatise with the French government at Fontainebleau on September 14, 1946, agreeing to the presence of the French army in North Vietnam. In the struggle against French colonization the legacy of Ngo Dinh Diem, a Catholic and the first president of the Republic of Vietnam, is incontrovertible, whatever political opinion one may have about his later political activities and his family.

In terms of culture, mention has been made of the contribution of seventeenth-century Jesuit missionaries (in particular, Alexandre de Rhodes) to the invention of the national script. To this linguistic achievement must be added the composition by later missionaries of dictionaries (e.g., those by Bishops Pierre Pigneau de Béhaine and Jean-Louis Taberd), grammars and ethnographic studies (e.g., those by Léopold Cadière), and catechetical and spiritual treatises (e.g., those by Girolamo Maiorica in the demotic script).

Vietnamese Catholics have enriched their country's cultural treasure with their own achievements. In literature, Petrus Truong Vinh Ky (1837–98) has left a large body of works in Vietnamese (in both the demotic and national scripts) and in French; Han Mac Tu (1912–40) invented a whole new genre of religious poetry. In linguistics, Paulus Huinh Tinh Cua (1834–1907) contributed an important dictionary and Le Van Ly (1913–92) a path-breaking work on Vietnamese grammar. In philosophy, the works of Kim Dinh (1914–95) provided the foundation for a Vietnamese

Confucianism. In social reform, Nguyen Truong To (1832–71) sought to modernize Vietnam with his fourteen ground-breaking proposals. In architecture, the cathedral of Phat Diem, built by Father Petrus Tran Luc (1825–99), popularly known as Cu Sau, is an outstanding achievement. We will forego mentioning the contributions of legions of still-living Vietnamese Catholics, especially in the Diaspora, to all fields of human endeavor, including literature, philosophy, theology, science, engineering, medicine, music, and the plastic arts. All of these contributions add to the richness and diversity of the Vietnamese culture.

More than any other religious organization, the Vietnamese Catholic Church has made a lasting impact in education and social service. In education, the contribution of male religious, in particular the La Salle Christian Brothers, is immense. In medical and social services, the work of female religious is unparalleled. Even during the difficult years since 1975, the Vietnamese Catholic Church continues, quietly and heroically, its ministry of love and service to its people, Catholic and non-Catholic alike. Deserving special notice is its care for the victims of leprosy in more than thirty centers throughout the country.

As with any Asian country, Vietnam is not immune from the political and economic effects of globalization with its twin driving forces of democracy and free market capitalism. In addition to the social upheavals caused by globalization, there are moral and cultural challenges facing Vietnam and Vietnamese Catholicism, not unlike those confronting Vietnamese-American Catholics. The following two chapters outline some of these, and the lessons from the experiences of Vietnamese-American Catholics can be illuminating also for Vietnamese Catholicism in general.

Chapter 6

WHO ARE VIETNAMESE-AMERICAN CATHOLICS?

LIVING THE CHRISTIAN FAITH IN THE NEW WORLD

Vietnamese people are now spread around the world. Among these, 550,000 are Catholic, 300,000 of whom reside in the United States. This chapter first gives a survey of these Vietnamese-American Catholics. Next, it suggests some concrete ways in which a Vietnamese theology can be developed. Finally, it indicates how Vietnamese-American Catholics can continue to practice their faith in their new homeland.

Vietnamese-American Catholics

Of a little more than one million Vietnamese Americans 30 percent are Catholic, compared to 8 percent in Vietnam. They form 150 communities or missions, 10 quasi-parishes, and 35 parishes. There are 600 priests, secular, and religious; 50 permanent deacons; 300 perpetually professed sisters; and 350 sisters in temporary vows. There are 50 religious orders or societies. Religious societies with a large Vietnamese membership include the Society of Divine Word (SVD) and the Society of Jesus (SJ).

States with a large concentration of Vietnamese Catholics are, in descending order: California (Orange County, San Jose, Los Angeles, San Diego, San Bernardino-River Side); Texas (Houston, Dallas/Fort Worth, Arlington, Austin); Louisiana (New Orleans); Georgia (Atlanta); Massachusetts (Boston); Illinois (Chicago, Joliet); Michigan (Grand Rapids, Detroit, Lansing); Oregon (Portland); Pennsylvania (Philadelphia); Washington (Seattle); Virginia (Arlington, Richmond); Maryland (Silver Spring); Washington, D.C.; and North Carolina (Raleigh-Durham) and South Carolina (Charleston).

Vietnamese-American Catholics are represented by a nonprofit organization called *Lien Doan Cong Giao Viet Nam Tai Hoa Ky* (Federation of Vietnamese Catholics in the United States of America) that has a central committee. The federation is composed of three groups: Community of Priests and Male Religious; Community of Female Religious; and Community of Lay Faithful. The federation is divided into eight geographical regions. Each region has an administrative committee of priests and religious and a committee of lay faithful. The federation of each region meets once a year; the community of priests and male and female religious meets once every two years; the community of lay faithful meets once a year; and a national meeting of the federation takes place every four years.

In addition to this organization, there is a Vatican-sponsored Office of Coordination of the Apostolate for Vietnamese Catholics in the Diaspora that periodically organizes activities of various kinds (e.g., pilgrimage to Rome) in which a great number of Vietnamese-American Catholics take part.

Pastorally, Vietnamese Catholics are served in parishes, quasi-parishes, or communities. Most dioceses with a large group of Vietnamese Catholics have one or more "Vietnamese" parishes, with a Vietnamese pastor, or several quasi-parishes, with a Vietnamese administrator (e.g., Dallas/Fort Worth, Galveston-Houston, New Orleans, Washington, D.C., Arlington, Virginia, etc.). When the number of Vietnamese Catholics is not large enough and/or too scattered, a Vietnamese priest is appointed to serve several different communities throughout the diocese. However, in California, even though the communities of Vietnamese Catholics are very large, the common practice of most dioceses is not to establish "Vietnamese" parishes but to have a Vietnamese Pastoral Center to coordinate various activities for Vietnamese Catholics and to have Vietnamese priests serve the Vietnamese Catholics at the parishes where they are pastors or associate pastors.

Each Vietnamese parish, quasi-parish, or community typically has a pastoral council to assist the Vietnamese priest in his ministry. In addition, several organizations and pious modalities are very active, such as Catholic Mothers, Devotion to the Sacred Heart, Eucharistic Youth, Cursillo, the Blue Army, Legio Mariae, Fatima Apostolate, Ignatian Spiritual Exercises, Boy and Girls Scouts, and Charismatic Catholics. Beyond regular activities common to every parish such as the catechumenate, religious education, instruction for sacramental reception (i.e., First Communion, Confirmation, and Marriage), and adult ongoing formation, there are cultural activities such as classes in Vietnamese language and culture.

Nationally, each August there is an annual Marian Festival organized in Carthage, Missouri, by the Society of Mary Co-Redemptrix, a congregation founded by a Vietnamese priest, Father Tran Dinh Thu. The festival regularly attracts some forty thousand participants every year and is an excellent opportunity for religious and cultural formation.

Vietnamese-American Catholics are well served by a number of popular magazines, chief among which are *Dan Chua* (People of God), *Trai Tim Duc Me* (The Heart of

Mary), *Duc Me hand Cuu Giup* (Our Lady of Perpetual Help), *Hiep Nhat* (Unity), *Dan Than* (Engagement), *Dat Me* (Motherland), and *Dien Dan Giao Dan* (Forum of Lay Catholics). In addition, the Institute of Vietnamese Philosophy and Religion, founded in 1998, offers annual conferences and publishes a scholarly journal on subjects related to theology and philosophy. There are also three valuable scholarly journals: *Dinh Huong* (Orientation), *Tap Tuyen Than Hoc* (Selections of Theology), and *Tap San Triet Dao* (Journal of Vietnamese Philosophy and Religion).

Vietnamese Theology: A New Way of Doing Theology

One of the many urgent needs of Vietnamese Catholicism is to develop a truly inculturated theology that takes into account Vietnamese history, culture, and religions.

This Vietnamese theology is of course an extremely complex and all-encompassing enterprise. A Vietnamese theology is not simply a different theology but also a new way of doing theology. To construct an authentically Vietnamese theology is therefore not a matter of simply adjusting a few key Christian doctrines to the Vietnamese mentality and context while preserving the way of doing theology customary in the West. On the contrary, an authentically Vietnamese theology must adopt a new starting point, new resources, a new way of interpreting the Christian sources (hermeneutics), and a new way of relating theological understanding to the practice of the Christian faith (praxis).

This is not the place to discuss at length the methodology of a Vietnamese theology, but four points need to be stressed. First, a Vietnamese theology must start from the socio-political, economic, cultural, and religious Vietnamese context, and not from some abstract text or doctrine. Hence, the context is not something external to theology to which Christian doctrines are adapted. Rather, contextual realities become resources for theology insofar as they embody and manifest the presence and action of God and God's Spirit.

Second, the resources for a Vietnamese theology must include everything we have discussed in chapters 1 through 5: Vietnam's myths of origin; its struggles against foreign domination and for self-determination; its heroes and heroines; its philosophical worldview; its material, ideational, and performative culture together with its cultural code; its religions; its customs and festivals; its popular literature, in particular its proverbs and folksongs; its literary classics; its artistic monuments. In addition, a Vietnamese theology must also include the experiences of over 3 million Vietnamese expatriates, their "joys and hopes," their sufferings and sorrows, their successes and failures in their new countries. All this is the grist that must be brought to the theological mill to produce a new Vietnamese theology with its own substance and flavor, shape, and color, all the while harmonious with the good news proclaimed by Jesus.

Third, a Vietnamese theology will bring the results of its analysis of all these resources into a critical correlation with the explicitly Christian sources, namely, the Bible and Tradition. In this process, Vietnamese theology will adopt a new way of interpreting the Bible and Tradition, by using the methods of reading sacred texts followed by other religions, by highlighting the liberative themes explicit or implicit in the Bible and Tradition, by allowing the Christian Bible and Tradition and the sacred texts of other religions to throw light on one another and to correct one another, and by privileging narratives, bodily gestures, and arts as a particularly effective way of interpreting a written text among Asians.

Fourth, a Vietnamese theology will move beyond these two stages of theological reflection—socio-political and cultural analysis and critical interpretation—to the third stage, namely, critical practice (praxis). It must show how these reflections should lead to a more faithful practice of the Christian faith, in conformity with God's preferential love for the poor and the marginalized, and to a more authentic worship of God. A Vietnamese theology must necessarily be both active contemplation and contemplative action. And this critical practice will in turn bring new materials and resources to the theological mill to generate another cycle of critical analysis and interpretation and praxis. In what follows, using the methodology just outlined, I offer very tentative reflections on how certain key Christian doctrines can be reformulated in the context of Vietnamese culture.

The Trinity: Heaven, Humanity, Earth

As we saw in chapter 2, one of the major insights of Vietnamese *tam tai* (three-element) philosophy is that Heaven, Earth, and Humanity are intrinsically related and even interdependent. Each is assigned a specific function: Heaven gives birth; Earth nurtures; and Humanity harmonizes.

It is possible to correlate the Christian doctrine of the Trinity with the Vietnamese *tam tai* philosophy. In their relationships to us and their activities in history (what theologians call the Economic Trinity), the three Divine Persons may be correlated with Heaven, Humanity, and Earth. God the Father, the Almighty, "maker of heaven and earth, of all that is seen and unseen," is correlated with Heaven, which gives birth. God the Father, the Almighty, is *Ong Troi* (Mr. Heaven) who, according to the Vietnamese belief, is the supreme being who is transcendent and all-powerful and who gives birth, rules, and directs the world through his will.

God the Son is correlated with Humanity, whose function is to harmonize. In taking human flesh and in his suffering and death, the Son harmonizes or reconciles his fellow human beings, his sisters and brothers, with Heaven, God the Father. As we will see below, the Son is not just a human being among others, he is also the Eldest Son and the Ancestor, who has special functions and duties that are crucial in the Vietnamese traditional family system.

God the Holy Spirit is correlated with Earth, whose function is to nurture. Like Mother-Earth who feeds humans through what she produces, the Spirit nurtures us through the gift of himself as love and grace and enables us to look up to and move toward Heaven, God the Father.

Just as Heaven, Earth, and Humanity are interconnected and interdependent, so the three Divine Persons, in what theologians call the Immanent Trinity, are united to each other in their life and activities. Because the three activities of giving birth, harmonizing, and nurturing are really distinct, though mutually related, the three Divine Persons who perform them as their distinct functions are distinct from each other (and therefore the error that theologians term *modalism* is avoided). Furthermore, since all three functions are equally necessary, the three Divine Persons who perform them are equal to each other (and therefore the error that theologians term *subordinationism* is also avoided). Finally, because harmonizing and nurturing are rooted in giving birth, just as the Son is born of the Father and the Spirit proceeds from the Father, the three Divine Persons do not constitute three gods but rather are one God, one because of the one life-giving source, God the Father (and therefore the error that theologians call *tritheism*, too, is avoided).

This trinitarian theology is but one of the many possible ways of understanding (not explaining) the Christian mystery of the Trinity. It has the advantage of starting from the Vietnamese experiences of Heaven, Earth, and Humanity in their lives. It helps to clarify how the doctrine of the

Trinity is not a mathematical puzzle of one being three and three being one, much less an unintelligible absurdity, but a reality experienced in Vietnamese daily life. These concrete experiences of giving birth, harmonizing, and nurturing can be critically correlated with God's threefold activity of creation, redemption, and sanctification that the Christian faith narrates and celebrates. Lastly, in this way, the Economic Trinity and the Immanent Trinity are shown to be identical; the Economic Trinity leads us to know the Immanent Trinity because the former is the visible manifestation and historical realization of the latter.

Vietnamese Images of Jesus

In his apostolic exhortation *Ecclesia in Asia* (November 6, 1999), which he promulgated after the Asian Synod (April 19–May 14, 1998), Pope John Paul II notes that the Synod encouraged Asian theologians in "their delicate work of developing an inculturated theology, especially in the area of Christology" (no. 22). Earlier he cites the "images of Jesus which would be intelligible to Asian minds and cultures and, at the same time, faithful to Scripture and Tradition" that have been suggested by the Synod: "Jesus Christ as the Teacher of Wisdom, the Healer, the Liberator, the Spiritual Guide, the Enlightened One, the Compassionate Friend of the Poor, the Good Samaritan, the Good Shepherd, the Obedient One" (no. 20). Of course, some of these images are biblical and familiar, others astounding, especially when translated into the local idioms, such as "The Spiritual Guide" (Jesus as the Guru) and "The Enlightened One" (Jesus as the Buddha).

From Vietnamese culture, I would highlight two images of Jesus: Jesus as the Firstborn Son and Eldest Brother and Jesus as the Ancestor. In addition, in the Vietnamese-American context, Jesus can also be seen as the Immigrant Par Excellence.

Jesus as the Firstborn Son and Eldest Brother

As explained in chapters 2 and 3, according to Vietnamese ethics, filial piety is the most fundamental virtue, and it is exercised by taking care of parents and fulfilling their wishes while they are alive, and after their deaths, by the practice of ancestor veneration. Though the duties of filial piety, including ancestor veneration, are incumbent upon all children, the eldest son is charged with overseeing their proper fulfillment. In the Gospels Jesus is often presented as the firstborn son (Luke 2:7; Matt 1:25). After the incident in the Temple, he returned home with his parents and there "was obedient to them" (Luke 2:51). He always behaved toward his mother with respect and tender love, praising her for doing God's will (Luke 8:21), carrying out her wishes (John 2:1–12), and looking after her well-being (John 19:26–27). With regard to his heavenly Father, Jesus is depicted as the model of filial piety, particularly in his obedience to his Father's will: "My food is to do the will of him who sent me and to complete his work" (John 4:34; see also 5:30).

As the Firstborn Son, Jesus is also the Eldest Brother. Because we have been adopted by God as God's children, we have a share in Jesus' unique sonship and become his sisters and brothers: "Those whom he [God] foreknew he also predestined to be conformed to the image of his Son, in order that he might be the firstborn within a large family" (Rom 8:29). Because Jesus was the Firstborn Son and the Eldest Brother, in the name of all of us, whom "Jesus is not ashamed to call brothers" (Heb 2:11), he offers his perfect sacrifice of filial obedience to God, his and our Father (Heb 1:5; 12:1–11). In this sense, Jesus as the High Priest can be compared to the Vietnamese emperor who on New Year's Day, in his capacity of the "Son of Heaven" and in the name of the people, offers the *Te Nam Giao* to Heaven.

Jesus as the Ancestor

In addition to being the Firstborn Son and the Eldest Brother, Jesus is also an Ancestor, or better still, the Proto-Ancestor (First Ancestor). By his death and resurrection Jesus became an ancestor: he is no longer dead but is alive among his brothers and sisters, just as parents, though dead, are present among their children. The New Testament repeatedly presents Jesus as the new Adam, the ancestor of the new human race. Luke's genealogy of Jesus explicitly links him to Adam. Mark describes how, like the old Adam, Jesus dwelt among the animals (Mark 1:13). Behind the Pauline hymn (Phil 2:2–11), there is an implied contrast between the old Adam, who sought to make himself equal to God, and Jesus the new Adam, who did not jealously cling to it. Besides these implicit references, there are texts such as 1 Corinthians 15:45–49 and Romans 5:12–21 that explicitly oppose the first Adam to the present Adam, the former marked by filial impiety (disobedience) and the latter by filial piety (obedience), the former a bad ancestor who brought about death and condemnation, and the latter a good ancestor who restored life and justification. Lastly, as the Proto-Ancestor, Jesus is now receiving the worship of his spiritual descendants, just as dead parents receive the veneration of their children.

Jesus as the Immigrant and Border-Crosser Par Excellence

In the context of Vietnamese-American Catholicism, Jesus can also be presented as the Immigrant Par Excellence. Immigrants, and more so, refugees, exist at the margins of two societies, the native one that they are forced to flee from and the strange one to which they must acculturate. They live betwixt and between two worlds, belonging to neither fully. Existentially, they are border-crossers, and the borders they have to cross are multiple and complex: geographical, political, economic, social, linguistic, psychological, cultural, and spiritual. Vietnamese Americans are viewed as not sufficiently Vietnamese. They are designated as *viet kieu* (foreign Vietnamese) when they go back to Vietnam. On the other hand, in the United States, American Vietnamese are regarded as not sufficiently American. Most often they are classified as "resident aliens," and even after having lived many years in America and having acquired citizenship, they still are, on account of their physical makeup, taken by many non-Asian Americans as foreigners. Even their political loyalty to the United States is put in doubt, and their civil rights systematically violated with impunity, especially when their former countries are in conflict with America, as the Japanese Americans' internment during World War II reminds us.

Paradoxically, however, immigrants and refugees, while belonging to neither their former nor their new country, do belong to both. Vietnamese Americans are neither fully American nor fully Vietnamese, but they are also *both* American *and* Vietnamese. In their existence they try to bring about something new: a hyphenated American Vietnamese and Vietnamese American. They try to be beyond both purely American and purely Vietnamese. They live and move and have their being in both worlds.

In light of this unique experience, they are in a position to understand Jesus as the Immigrant and the Border-Crosser Par Excellence, in his incarnation, ministry, and death and resurrection. The mystery of the Word of God made flesh in Jesus can certainly be viewed as an act of border-crossing. Essentially, it is the culmination of that primordial border-crossing by which the Triune God steps out of himself and eternity and crosses into the other, namely, the world of space and time, which God brings into existence by this very act of crossing. In the incarnation, the border that was crossed is not only that which separates the eternal and the temporal, the invisible and the visible, spirit and matter, but more specifically, the divine and the human, with the latter's reality of soul and body.

In this divine crossing over to the human, the border between the divine nature and the human nature of Jesus functions as the marker constituting the distinct identity of each. One is not transmuted into the other, nor confused with it; rather, the two natures are to be acknowledged "without confusion, without change." As the Council of Chalcedon teaches: "The distinction between the natures was never abolished by their union, but rather the character proper to each of the two natures was preserved as they came together in one person *[prosopon]* and one hypostasis."

On the other hand, the same border is no longer a barrier preventing God and the human from joining together. Indeed, by crossing the divine-human border, the Logos transforms the barrier into a frontier and creates a new reality, Jesus of Nazareth, whose humanity the Logos assumes and makes it his own, so that, as the Council of Chalcedon teaches, his two natures—divine and human—are united with each other "without division, without separation." In this humanity the Logos now exists in a new way, not available to him before the incarnation, and this historical mode of existence, in time and space, and above all, as we will see, in suffering and death, now belongs to God's eternal and trinitarian life itself.

Thus, in the incarnation as border-crossing, the boundaries are preserved as identity markers but at the same time they are overcome as barriers and transformed into frontiers from which a totally new reality, a *mestizaje,* emerges: the divine and human reconciled and harmonized with each other into one single reality. Like Jesus, immigrants are constantly challenged to cross all kinds of borders, and out of the best of each group of people these borders divide and separate, to create a new human family characterized by harmony and reconciliation.

A border-crosser at the very roots of his being, Jesus performed his ministry of announcing and ushering in the kingdom of God always at the places where borders meet and hence at the margins of the two worlds separated by their borders. He was a "marginal Jew." He crossed these borders back and forth repeatedly and freely, be they geographical, racial, sexual, social, economic, political, cultural, or religious. What is new about his message about the kingdom of God—which is good news to some and scandal to others—is that for him it removes all borders, both natural and man-made, as barriers and is absolutely all-inclusive. Jews and non-Jews, men and women, the old and the young, the rich and the poor, the powerful and the weak, the healthy and the sick, the clean and the impure, the righteous and the sinners, and all other imaginable categories of peoples and groups—Jesus invited them all to enter into the house of his merciful and forgiving Father. Even in his preferential option for the poor Jesus did not abandon and exclude the rich and the powerful. They, too, are called to conversion and to live a just, all-inclusive life.

Standing between the two worlds, excluding neither but embracing both, Jesus was able to be fully inclusive of both. But this also means that he is the Marginal Person Par Excellence. People at the center of any society or group as a rule possess wealth, power, and influence. As the threefold temptation shows, Jesus, the Border-Crosser and the Dweller at the Margins, renounced precisely these three things. Because he was at the margins in his teaching and miracle-working, Jesus creates a new and different center, the center constituted by the meeting of the borders of the many and diverse worlds, often in conflict with one another, each with its own center that relegates the "other" to the margins. It is at this margin-center that marginal people meet one another. In Jesus, the margin where he lived became the center of a new society without borders and barriers, reconciling all peoples, "Jew or Greek...slave or free...male or female" (Gal 3:28). Strangers and guests as they are, immigrants are invited to become marginal people, to dwell at the margins of societies with marginal(ized) people, like Jesus, so as to be able to create with them new all-inclusive centers of reconciliation and harmony.

Jesus' violent death on the cross was a direct result of his border-crossing and ministry at the margins, which posed a serious threat to the interests of those occupying the economic, political, and religious center. Even the form of his death, crucifixion, indicates that Jesus was an outcast, and he died, as the Letter to Hebrews says, "outside the city gate...[and] outside the camp" (13:12–13). Symbolically, however, hung between Heaven and Earth, at the margins of both worlds, Jesus acted as the mediator and intercessor between God and humanity.

But even in death Jesus did not remain within the boundaries of what death means: failure, defeat, destruction. By his resurrection he crossed the borders of death into a new life, thus bringing hope where there was despair, victory where there was vanquishment, freedom where there was slavery, and life where there was death. In this way, the borders of death become frontiers to life in abundance. Like Jesus, Vietnamese Americans have to live out the dynamics of death and resurrection, or, to use the words of Philippians 2:6–11, of self-emptying and exaltation.

A Vietnamese Mary:
The Mother of Compassion

Like many other countries, Vietnam claims to have had Marian apparitions. So far there are two locations where our Lady is said to have appeared, La Vang and Tra Kieu, the former by far the more famous of the two. Compared with Western apparitions, such as Lourdes and Fatima, there is no historical documentation for these two apparitions but only unverifiable oral tradition. Furthermore, our Lady did not appear to identifiable individuals (like Bernadette Soubirous or Lucia, Francesco, and Jacinta) but to a large group of anonymous people. Nor was there a doctrinal message conveyed (like Mary's Immaculate Conception) or a spiritual practice recommended (like reform of life, recital of the Rosary, and devotion to the Heart of Mary). Both alleged apparitions have one thing in common: our Lady is said to have appeared during the persecution of Catholics and promised them maternal protection.

Our Lady of La Vang

The years 1798–1800, under the reign of King Canh Thinh (1792–1802), were very hard for Catholics. The king suspected that his opponent Nguyen Anh was being assisted by the French bishop Pigneau de Béhaine (d. 1799), who had recruited French officers and arms to help Nguyen Anh reestablish his dynasty. Fearful that Catholics would collude with his enemies, the king ordered them to be killed as a preventive measure. La Vang was a small Catholic village, with about 150 inhabitants, about 80 miles north of Hue, the ancient capital, in the Quang Tri province. There are two accounts, one Catholic, the other Buddhist, of why the village became a Marian site.

According to the Catholic version, during Canh Thinh's persecution, several Catholics from the nearby parish of Co Vuu fled to La Vang. There, in spite of severe sufferings, they gathered every evening under a banian tree to recite the Rosary. One evening, according to the tradition, a lady of great beauty appeared to them, clad in white and surrounded by light, holding the infant Jesus in her arms, with two charming boys holding torches standing at her sides. The lady walked back and forth several times in front of the Christians, her feet touching the ground. Even the non-Christians who were there saw the vision. Then the lady stopped and addressed them in a sweet voice: "My children, what you have asked of me, I have granted you, and henceforth, whoever will come here to pray to me, I will listen to them." Then she vanished.

The Buddhist version, called "The Pagoda of the Three Villages," runs as follows. There were three villages near La Vang, namely, Co Thanh, Thach Han, and Ba Tru. The Buddhists there heard that a lady called Thien Mu (literally: The Heavenly Lady) had appeared in La Vang under the banian tree (which is considered a sacred tree) and that those who went there to pray were miraculously healed. During the persecution of Catholics under Emperor Ming Mang (1820–40), the Buddhists took over the place and built a pagoda in honor of the Buddha. The night after the dedication of the pagoda, so the story goes, the leaders of the three villages had a dream in which the Buddha appeared to them and told them to remove his statue from La Vang, because, he said, there was a lady more powerful than him occupying the place. The following day they went to the pagoda and saw that the Buddha statue and its ornaments had been moved outside and so they brought them in. Again, that night they had the same dream and received the same message. As a result, the Buddhists donated the pagoda to the Catholics, who converted it into the first chapel of Our Lady of La Vang.

What historical validity is to be attached to both accounts is impossible to determine. The Vietnamese hierarchy has not officially pronounced on the historicity of Mary's apparition at La Vang. Nevertheless, there is no doubt that Vietnamese Catholics regard La Vang as a sacred site. In 1901 a small chapel was built there and was blessed by Louis Casper, bishop of Hue, during a solemn procession in which, somewhat incongruously, a statue of the French Notre-Dame des Victoires was honored. Since then, every three years there has been an organized pilgrimage to La Vang, except when impeded by war. In 1924 a larger sanctuary was built to replace the chapel, now too small for the huge crowd. In 1959 it was raised to the rank of minor basilica by Blessed Pope John XXIII and became the national Marian center of pilgrimage. Under the current communist government, travels to La Vang have been severely restricted. Nevertheless, the bicentennial commemoration of our Lady's apparition at La Vang in 1988 was attended by a huge number of Catholics, from both North and South, with Cardinal Phan Dinh Tung, archbishop of Hanoi, presiding as the special legate of Pope John Paul II.

Our Lady of Tra Kieu

In 1885 the Vietnamese Catholic Church was afflicted with another wave of persecution. After the death of Emperor Tu Duc (1883), a proroyal movement called *Can Vuong* was initiated by the young emperor Ham Nghi, who acceded to the throne in 1884, to fight against the French colonial power. The movement practically ended when Ham Nghi was arrested by the French in 1888 and exiled to Algeria. It was composed mainly of court officials sharing Ham Nghi's liberation program. Another movement called *Van Than* (literati), many members of which joined the Can Vuong movement, instigated a campaign of *binh Tay sat Ta* (literally: destroying the West and killing the false religion), code words for the French and the Vietnamese Catholics, respectively. Tra Kieu, a small village of some nine hundred inhabitants, in the province of Quang Nam, south of Hue, had a tiny parish.

On September 1, 1885, the parish with its pastor, Father Jean Bruyère, was surrounded by the *Van Than* army who, however, did not attack until the following day. The Catholics were desperate, outnumbered three to one, and with very few weapons. Father Bruyère urged them to place their confidence in Mary by putting a statue of Mary on the table with a candle on each side. While the young men went out to fight, old people, women, and children recited the Rosary. The *Van Than* army, despite its overwhelming force, was held at bay for several days. Frustrated by their defeat, the *Van Than* decided to bring in canons and began shooting at the church. However, all their canons, to the *Van Than's* consternation, missed their easy mark. A military mandarin later confessed that he saw a beautiful lady, dressed in white, standing on top of the church, and that he tried to hit her with the canons but always missed. The soldiers kept saying aloud for two days that this lady stood on top of the church and that, try as they might, they could never hit her.

On September 21, the *Van Than* decided to carry out a final assault on the parish. The Catholics, on their part, decided that the best defense was offense, in spite of great risks because of their numerical inferiority and lack of weapons. They made a sortie and attacked the *Van Than* troops who were occupying the two hills overlooking the village. Again, according to M. Geffroy, the *Van Than* used elephants to attack the Catholics, but the animals refused to move. The riders explained that the elephants were terrified because there were thousands of children, dressed in white and red, coming down from the bamboo trees and marching with the Catholics toward them. Then one of the Catholics shot and killed one of the literati in charge of the *Van Than* troops, which caused them to run away in total disarray. The Catholics attributed their improbable victory to the protection of Mary.

As with La Vang, there is no way to validate the *Van Than's* vision of the lady dressed in white and standing on top of the church to protect it and of troops of children dressed in white and red coming down from the bamboo trees to join forces with the Catholics at Tra Kieu. Nevertheless, the Vietnamese Catholics did not hesitate to attribute to Mary's miraculous intervention their victory over their enemies whose number and weapons were overwhelming. In 1898 a chapel was built in Tra Kieu, dedicated to Mary Help of Christians, and in 1959 and 1971 pilgrimages to this Marian sanctuary were organized with a large number of participants.

Mary: The Mother of Mercy

In light of these apparitions and in the context of Vietnamese culture, a portrait of Mary that represents her as the Mother of Mercy can be extremely attractive and of great pastoral relevance.

1. As is clear from the above narratives, Mary's alleged apparitions at La Vang and Tra Kieu both occurred in the context of persecution, which is very different from that of other major Marian apparitions such as those at Lourdes and Fatima. Mary appeared at La Vang and Tra Kieu as a protective mother, full of love and mercy for her suffering children. She did not threaten apocalyptic divine punishment if the Vietnamese people did not repent, nor did she require them to do anything in return for her favors. On the contrary, out of gratuitous and merciful love, she liberated them and promised to listen favorably to those who would pray to her. In other words, she is the figure of pure mercy and compassion. She

suffered with and protected the Vietnamese Catholics because they suffered.

It is perhaps this figure of Mary as the embodiment of divine mercy that powerfully attracts the Vietnamese, Catholics and non-Christian alike, to her. It is well known that the Buddha is often presented as a man of infinite compassion for suffering humankind, and that it was out of this compassion that he taught the Eightfold Path that would lead humans out of suffering and toward enlightenment. Three of the four divine attitudes or virtues *(brahmavihas)* that the Buddha stresses as necessary to achieve Buddhahood or enlightenment have to do with this quality of mercy and compassion: *metta,* sometimes translated as "friendship," is a selfless, universal, all-expansive love; *karuna* is compassion for all living beings in their suffering, with no sense of superiority over them; and *mudita* is an altruistic joy in the success or welfare of others. In particular, *karuna* is not an emotional sympathy, a mere feeling of pity, or a helpless vicarious suffering for others but compassion that leads to positive action on behalf of one's fellow sufferers.

In Vietnam, where Mahayana Buddhism is prevalent, the virtue of *karuna* is highly stressed, as equal to wisdom *(prjña)*. It is in this tradition that we have the figure of Avalokitesvara, a bodhisattva whose infinite compassion for suffering beings makes him/her postpone his/her own freedom from suffering and delusion until he/she can save all other beings from suffering as well. This is not the place to discuss the historical origins and the different manifestations of this extremely popular Buddhist figure, in India as well as in China, Japan, and Korea. Suffice it to point out that in Vietnam, as well as in China, Japan, and Korea, there is the female figure of Kwan-Yin (in Japan: Kannon), much beloved not only by Buddhists but also by the general populace. She is thought to be like mother, sister, friend, and queen, always listening to the cries for help (the word *Kwan-Yin* means "regarder of sounds," that is, the voices of the suffering). She is the first bodhisattva to whom laypeople turn in time of trouble, and whom they seek to worship in gratitude for blessings received. Her statue is displayed in all Buddhist pagodas as well as in Taoist temples. In Vietnam, she is connected with the story of Thi Kinh, which we have narrated in chapter 3, and is represented as a woman holding a child and crushing a toad with her right foot.

Given this cultural and religious context, it is no wonder that the Vietnamese Catholics readily see in Mary the figure who embodies divine compassion and mercy and who is always ready to assist them. Love of and devotion to Mary as the Mother of Mercy, for Vietnamese Catholics, is a natural extension of their love of and devotion to the merciful Quan Âm Thi Kính. Interestingly, Pope John Paul II, in his encyclical *Dives in misericordia* on God the Father, describes Mary as the "Mother of Mercy" who has "*the deepest knowledge of God's mercy.* She knows its price, she knows how great it is. In this sense, we call her the *Mother of Mercy:* our Lady of Mercy, or Mother of Divine Mercy" (no. 9.2).

Furthermore, this Mariology echoes well the concerns of feminist theology, which sees in Mary a Jewish woman who makes an option for the poor, and whose Magnificat is a magna carta for the liberation of humans from all forms of oppression, especially those of patriarchialism and androcentrism. This view is confirmed by Pope John Paul II who, in his encyclical *Redemptoris Mater,* sees Mary's Magnificat as an expression of her love for the poor: "The Church's *love of preference for the poor* is wonderfully inscribed in Mary's *Magnificat*...Drawing from Mary's heart, from the depth of her faith expressed in the words of the *Magnificat,* the Church renews ever more effectively in herself the awareness that *the truth about God who saves,* the truth about God who is the source of every gift, *cannot be separated from the manifestation of his love of preference for the poor and humble,* that love which, celebrated in the *Magnificat,* is later expressed in the words and works of Jesus" (*Redemptoris Mater,* no. 37.3).

2. The second component of a Vietnamese Mariology is the issue of power. From the accounts of the two Marian apparitions in Vietnam it is clear that Mary's merciful interventions were powerful and effective. The beleaguered Vietnamese Catholics were delivered from their persecutors. Mary showed herself a merciful mother, but not a weak one. Mercy, as has been said above, is not a mere sense of pity or a sentimental sympathy (suffering-with). Rather, it moves the compassionate person to action. Mercy without powerful action on behalf of the suffering is empty and demeaning. Conversely, power without mercy, which, in the words of John Paul II, "has *the interior form of the love* that in the New Testament is called *agape*" *(Dives in misericordia,* no. 6.3), runs the risk of turning into dictatorship.

This figure of a powerful woman has much to recommend it to the Vietnamese people and is well represented in Vietnamese history and culture. This may explain why Marian devotion is also widely popular with Vietnamese men. It is true that Confucian morality, which was imposed on the Vietnamese by the Chinese during their thousand-year-long domination, is heavily patriarchal and androcentric. Women in a Confucian society are bound by Three Submissions *(tam tong):* when a child, she must submit to her father; in marriage, to her husband; in widowhood, to her eldest son. Their behavior is to be guided by Four Virtues *(tu duc)* that are designed to restrict women's role to the sphere of domesticity: assiduous housewifery *(cong),* pleasing appearance *(dung),* appropriate speech *(ngon),* and proper conduct *(hanh).*

Daily life and history in Vietnam, however, present a far different picture. As we saw in chapter 1, Vietnamese history is replete with female political and military leaders, among whom the most celebrated and beloved are the Trung sisters, Trung Trac and Trung Nhi, who led a revolution against the Chinese in AD 42. Another famous female leader is Trieu Au, who led an uprising against the Chinese in AD 248. Indeed, historians have argued that in the earliest Vietnamese society, called the Lac or Dong Son civilization (from the seventh century BC to the first century AD), women occupied a high position. Legally, Vietnamese women, compared with their Chinese counterparts, were in a far more favorable situation, accorded many important rights. In family life, women exert a far greater authority than their husbands; in fact, they are called *noi tuong* (internal general). The contributions of women to Vietnamese high culture are also notable, especially in literature.

Needless to say, given the central position of women in Vietnamese culture and history, in spite of the deeply ingrained Confucian patriarchalism and androcentrism, the figure of Mary as a powerful woman has profound implications for the struggle of Vietnamese women for equal rights and full human dignity. A Mariology that highlights the powerful role of Mary as a woman, together with her mercy and compassion, will be appealing to Vietnamese women and men.

3. The third component of a Vietnamese Mariology is interreligious dialogue. It is most interesting that in the Buddhist version of the origins of the Vietnamese devotion to Our Lady of La Vang it was the Buddhists who, at the Buddha's behest, voluntarily offered their pagodas to the Catholics who turned it into a Marian shrine. The relations between Buddhists and Catholics were apparently very amicable. Furthermore, according to this account, the statue of the Buddha was, as far as we know, not smashed as an idol

but simply moved to another place. In addition, in the Tra Kieu story, our Lady was not seen by the Catholics of the village but by the "pagans" who attacked them. Ironically, it was only through the testimony of the "unbelievers" that the "believers" knew that Mary had appeared and defended them! In a certain sense, Vietnamese Catholics owe their devotion to Mary to the "pagans," at least at Tra Kieu.

Dialogue with the followers of other faiths is not a luxury but an absolute necessity for Vietnamese Catholics. Indeed, it is an essential component of Christian mission in Vietnam, along with inculturation and liberation. This triple dialogue has been recognized by the Federation of Asian Bishops' Conferences to be the mode of Christian mission in Asia.

Given the number of common traits between Kwan-Yin and Mary, Mariology can serve as a fruitful starting point for an interreligious dialogue in Vietnam. Of course, a facile identification between the two figures is to be rejected. But that both of them allow us to imagine God as a loving, merciful, compassionate, saving, protecting, liberating Father for all the Vietnamese people, irrespective of their religious traditions, and that all Vietnamese are thereby called to promote a society of love, mercy, compassion, and freedom, this is beyond doubt. An authentic Vietnamese Mariology cannot but be an incentive for this interreligious dialogue.

Ancestor Veneration

As is well known, Vietnam, along with Korea and Japan, has been heavily influenced by China, especially in its Confucian culture. This influence is most visible in certain funerary rites and in the cult of ancestors. Needless to say, the Chinese Rites Controversy and the Roman condemnation of ancestor worship has affected Vietnamese Catholicism as well, profoundly and extensively, even until today.

Curiously, though *Propaganda Fide's Plane compertum est,* permitting the practice of ancestor veneration, was issued in 1939, it was not until 1964 that the Vietnamese hierarchy, somewhat unnecessarily, applied for its application to Vietnam. The request was approved on October 2, 1964. On June 14, 1964, the Vietnamese bishops in a communication entitled "The Veneration of Ancestors, National Heroes, and War Dead" spelled out the concrete norms to apply *Propaganda Fide's* instruction. In general, the bishops distinguished three kinds of acts, attitudes, and rituals: those that are clearly secular, patriotic, and social expressions of piety toward the ancestors, national heroes, and war dead; those that are clearly religious in nature and contrary to Catholic belief, smack of superstition, and are performed in places reserved for worship; and those that are of an ambiguous nature. The first kinds are not only permissible but are to be encouraged and promoted; the second are prohibited; and the third need to be examined according to the common local opinion: if they are generally thought to be of a nonreligious nature, they are permissible. If doubt concerning their nature persists, it is permissible to act according to one's conscience. If possible, explanations of one's intention should be given with due tact, or one can participate in a passive manner.

On April 12, 1974, the Vietnamese bishops issued another communication in which they specified a list of activities, attitudes, and rituals deemed permissible:

1. An altar dedicated to the veneration of the ancestors may be placed under the altar dedicated to God, provided that nothing superstitious such as the "white soul" (the white cloth representing the dead) is placed there.

2. Burning incense and lighting candles on the ancestral altar, and prostrating with joined hands in front of the altar

or the repository of the ancestors, are gestures of filial piety and veneration, and hence are permissible.

3. On death anniversaries it is permissible to present the dead person with "offerings of commemorative cult" according to local customs, provided that one eliminates superstitions such as burning paper money. It is also recommended that the offerings be reduced or changed to express more clearly their true meaning of respect and gratitude to the ancestors, for instance, flowers, fruits, incense, and lights.

4. During the marriage rites, the bride and groom are permitted to perform the "ceremony of veneration toward the ancestors" in front of the ancestral altar or the repository of the ancestors. These rituals are expressions of gratitude toward, recognition of, and self-presentation to the ancestors.

5. During the funerary rites, it is permissible to perform prostrations with joined hands before the corpse as well as to hold burning incense sticks in joined hands according to local customs, as a way to express veneration for the dead person, just as the Church permits the use of candles, incense, and inclination before the corpse.

6. It is permissible to participate in the ceremonies venerating the "lord of the place," who is usually called the "titulary genius," in the village community building, to express gratitude toward those whom history shows have earned the gratitude of the people, or the benefactors of the village, and not to express a superstitious belief in evil spirits and harmful ghosts.

In addition to the permission of these rituals of ancestor veneration outside of the liturgy, the Vietnamese bishops have introduced two properly liturgical innovations. The first is an expansion of the prayer for the dead in the Eucharistic Prayer of the Mass. In the second Eucharistic Prayer, instead of the simple formula "Remember our brothers and sisters who have gone to their rest in the hope of rising again," the Vietnamese memento of the dead reads: "Remember also the faithful, our brothers and sisters, who rest in peace in the expectation of the resurrection, and the dead who can only trust in your mercy. Remember in particular our *ancestors,* our parents and our friends who have left this world." Obviously, the explicit mention of ancestors is an attempt at inculturating ancestor veneration into the liturgy, with significant theological implications that will be detailed below.

The second liturgical innovation is the Masses for the celebration of the lunar New Year or Tet. Tet is celebrated for at least three days: the first is reserved for the cult of ancestors and the living parents, the second for near relatives, and the third for the dead. Alexandre de Rhodes had already attempted to Christianize Tet by suggesting that its three days be dedicated to the Trinity: the first day in memory of the benefits of creation and conservation, which is dedicated to God the Father; the second in thanksgiving for the inestimable benefit of redemption, which is dedicated to God the Son; and the third in humble gratitude to the Holy Spirit for the grace of being called to be a Christian.

Given the central position of Tet, it is not surprising that the Vietnamese bishops have undertaken to solemnize it with Eucharistic celebrations. Five Mass formulas have been composed to express the various meanings of Tet and are now in use: the first for the end of the year to give thanks and ask for forgiveness; the second for New Year's Eve to celebrate the passage into the new year *(giao thua);* the third for the first day of the new year to praise God and to ask for peace and prosperity; the fourth for the second day to pray for ancestors, grandparents, and parents; and the fifth for the third day to pray for the sanctification of labor.

For our present purpose the fourth formula is of special interest. Here are some of its significant prayers:

Collect: Father of mercies, you have commanded us to practice filial piety. Today, on New Year's Day, we have gathered to honor the memory of our ancestors, grandparents, and parents. Deign to reward abundantly those who have brought us into this world, nurtured us, and educated us. Help us live in conformity with our duties toward them...

Prayer over the Gifts: Lord, accept our offerings and bestow your graces abundantly upon our ancestors, grandparents, and parents, so that we may in our turn inherit their blessings...

Preface: As we look at things in the universe, we clearly see that every being has an origin and principle: birds have their nests, water its source, and the human person coming into this world has a father and mother. Moreover, thanks to your revelation, Father, we recognize that you are the creator of all things that exist and that you are our Father. You have given life to our ancestors, grandparents, and parents so that they may transmit it to us. You have also filled them with good things so we may inherit them by knowing you, adoring you, and serving you...

The inclusion of the veneration of ancestors into the Mass, and especially the mention of the term *ancestor* in the Eucharistic Prayer, mark a monumental step in liturgical inculturation in Vietnam. We have traveled a long way from the days of the Chinese Rites Controversy. Theologically, it is important, at least for two reasons. First, in mentioning the ancestors explicitly in the Eucharistic Prayer and in praying for them, the Vietnamese text does not distinguish between Christian ancestors and non-Christian ones (among Vietnamese Christians attending Mass there are many whose ancestors did not receive baptism). In the cult of ancestors, the ancestors are venerated not because they have been saved or were holy but simply because they are ancestors. In virtue of the physical bond with their descendants, the ancestors are bound to protect them, and the descendants to honor them. Furthermore, in describing the cult of ancestors, many Vietnamese bishops have used not only the word *to tien* (forebears) but also *thanh hien* (saint and sage) to refer to those who should receive this cult. Of course, they do not mean to say that these are "saints" in the Christian sense of being officially canonized, but clearly the old objection that the word *saint* should not be used of people like Confucius no longer holds, and of course there is no suggestion that non-Christian ancestors have been damned simply because they were not Christians.

Second, there is in the prayers cited above an affirmation that somehow the ancestors act as mediators of the blessings and graces that their descendants receive from God. The descendants are said to "inherit" them from their ancestors. Of course, in these prayers the ancestors are not directly asked to "intercede" for their descendants, since these prayers are not addressed to them, in contrast to those said in front of the ancestral altar at home. Theologically, of course, there can be no objection to asking someone, dead or alive, canonized or not, to intercede for oneself or others before God.

Chapter 7

WHAT LIES AHEAD FOR VIETNAMESE-AMERICAN CATHOLICS?

Pastoral Challenges and Opportunities

Vietnamese-American Catholics have brought to the United States and the American Catholic Church gifts of culture and faith. However, now no longer simply guests in a foreign land but citizens of a new nation and members of a new Church, they are challenged both to preserve what is best of their cultural and religious traditions and to appropriate values offered by America and the American Catholic Church.

Needless to say, in building their future Vietnamese-American Catholics face numerous challenges as well as enjoy many opportunities. This chapter highlights some of these opportunities and challenges in the hope that, like their predecessors from Africa, Europe, and Latin America, Vietnamese-American Catholics will be able to add their own riches to the common spiritual treasure of both the United States and the American Catholic Church.

Opportunities for Human Development and for Christian Life

No doubt what immigrants and refugees to the United States appreciate most are its respect for freedom and democracy and the opportunities life in a free and democratic country offers to each individual. Americans aspire—at least in principle—to four freedoms: from fear, from want, of speech, and, above all, of religion. Their rights and dignity are respected under the rule of law, and they are given plenty of scope to exercise the responsibilities of a citizen. Americans who have not suffered persecution and oppression may perhaps take these basic freedoms and democratic institutions for granted, but for immigrants and refugees, these are the very things they have risked life and limb for and they treasure them as opportunities for a full flourishing of their human potential. In particular, Vietnamese-American Catholics, who have experienced government restrictions on the public practice of their religion, welcome the separation of church and state and rejoice in the possibility of a full and untrammeled practice of their Christian faith.

The American Catholic Church, too, has provided Vietnamese-American Catholics with a welcoming home in which to live their faith and preserve their religious heritage. Except in extremely rare cases, Vietnamese-American Catholic clergy and laity have collaborated harmoniously with their ecclesiastical authorities. Furthermore, the consultative, almost democratic, style in which ministry is exercised in many parishes offers Vietnamese-American Catholics a unique opportunity to exercise their baptismal vocation and to break away from the more authoritarian and clerical model of church they have inherited.

Another aspect of the contemporary American Catholic Church that is also of great significance for Vietnamese-American Catholics is what has been referred to as "public Catholicism." Brought up in the religious ghetto of Vietnamese Catholicism that emphasizes the afterlife and individual salvation at the expense of the Church's ministry for justice and peace, Vietnamese-American Catholics are enriched by the American Church's commitment to be a transformative agent in society, especially in issues concerning peace, the economy, gender equality, and human life.

Another enriching opportunity offered by the American Catholic Church is its educational system, from the lowest to the highest levels, from parochial schools to universities, from occasional lectures to degree-granting programs. Long nurtured with question-and-answer catechisms and with little familiarity with the Bible and theology, Vietnamese-American Catholics would derive immense benefits from the opportunity of immersing themselves in the sources of the Christian faith and of obtaining a Catholic education.

Finally, the generosity with which American Catholics contribute to the welfare of their fellow members and the society at large through monetary donations and voluntary services is a much-needed example for Vietnamese-American Catholics. Traditionally taught to be concerned mainly if not exclusively about the welfare of their own families, they tend to neglect the wider common good of society and Church. They need to appropriate the American tradition of voluntarism and financial giving as opportunities to pay back society and Church for the many benefits they receive from them.

Challenges Ahead: Authentically American, Authentically Vietnamese, Authentically Catholic

These many and diverse opportunities are, from another point of view, also challenges for Vietnamese-American Catholics. In a nutshell, they are called to be authentically American, authentically Vietnamese, and authentically Catholic. Of course, there are at times tensions among these three, but there are and there should be no inner contradictions among them. Indeed, the genius of American Catholicism, as has been abundantly borne out by its history, is the ability to build a synthesis, however precarious and evolving, of these three basic elements: being a loyal citizen of the United States of America; being a faithful member of the one holy catholic and apostolic Church; and being a proud part of an ethnic group.

As *Americans,* Vietnamese-American Catholics are challenged to truly embrace the American option for the basic freedoms and democracy and to defend these freedoms and human rights for all, even for those Vietnamese who hold and express a different (e.g., communist) ideology. It would be the height of irony if, after having risked their lives to obtain the freedom of speech, Vietnamese Americans would themselves suppress the voice of those Vietnamese individuals they regard as Communists in their midst.

As *Vietnamese,* Vietnamese-American Catholics are challenged to preserve their language and teach it to their children; to celebrate their cultural and religious customs and festivals; to maintain their worldview of harmony among Heaven, Earth, and Humanity; and to fulfill the duties connected with their relationships, especially filial piety and ancestor veneration.

As *Catholics*, Vietnamese-American Catholics are challenged to continue their tradition of fostering numerous priestly and religious vocations; to promote practices of popular piety, in particular Marian devotion; to take pride in and imitate their martyrs; to carry out a real dialogue among the followers of different Vietnamese religions; to enhance the theological formation of their clergy and laity; to bring about a more collaborative style of ministry; and to engage more effectively in the work of justice and peace.

The Never-Ending Task of Inculturation

This task of becoming fully American, fully Vietnamese, and fully Catholic may be called *inculturation*. As pointed out in the previous chapter, while belonging fully to neither the American Church nor the Vietnamese Church, Vietnamese-American Catholics belong to both. Vietnamese-American Catholics live a Catholic life in a way no "pure" American Catholic can because of their indelible Asian religious traditions, and they live a Catholic life in a way no "pure" Asian Catholic is able to because of the distinctly American Catholic ethos that they have willy-nilly absorbed through sheer contiguity and symbiosis with the American society and Church.

But their betwixt-and-between position should not be viewed only as a negative asset causing marginalization but also as an opportunity to create a new way of being Catholic. Herein lies their unique contribution to the American Catholic Church.

But in order to accomplish this mission, where should they stand? What is their social location, the specific space they occupy within the American society and church? How should they be part of the societal and ecclesial realities? I suggest that we view the predicament of Vietnamese Americans as neither completely inside nor completely outside the American society but as belonging to both but not entirely, because they are *beyond* both.[1] The same thing should be said about Vietnamese-American Catholics. They are neither completely outside the American Catholic Church and their native Vietnamese Church nor completely inside them; they belong to both but not completely, because they are also *beyond* both. In other words, they live and move and have their being in the interstice between the American culture and their own, between the American Church and their Vietnamese Church. Because of this, there should be no attempt to absorb Vietnamese Americans into the American society and Vietnamese-American Catholics into the Catholic Church as though into a melting pot, in such a way that they would lose their distinct identities as both Asians and Asian Catholics. Nor should there be an attempt to keep them apart from the American society and the American Church in a kind of ghetto, marginalizing them from Church and society.

Furthermore, given the present reality of culture in the United States as globalized, conflictive, fragmented, and multiple, this space is not some preexisting no-man's-land, peacefully and definitively agreed on in advance by the powers that be of the two cultures and the two Churches. Rather, the interstice is to be carved out by Vietnamese-American Catholics themselves, in everyday living, by trial and error, in creative freedom, over the course of a lifetime. Its boundaries, quite porous to be sure, are ever shifting and are subject to being redrawn and renegotiated as new circumstances and needs arise. What remains indisputable is that Vietnamese-American Catholics have a right to this cultural and ecclesial interstitial space where they can fulfill their God-given mission of being the bridge between East and

---

1. On the concept of the immigrant as being "in-beyond," see Jung Young Lee, *Marginality: The Key to Multicultural Theology* (Minneapolis, MN: Fortress, 1995), 55–70.

West, between the Church of Vietnam and the Church of North America.

This does not mean that inculturation or interculturation is an arbitrary and haphazard process, bereft of theological and canonical guiding principles or without a supervising authority. Indeed, in the process of interculturation between the Vietnamese culture and the American culture, all three dimensions (i.e., signs, message, and codes) and all three levels of culture (i.e., the surface, the intermediate, and the ultimate), as explained in chapter 2, must be brought into play. Interculturation is the process whereby the American culture and the Vietnamese culture are brought into a reciprocal engagement in such a way that both of them are transformed from within. Essential to interculturation is the mutual criticism and enrichment between American culture and Vietnamese culture. The expressions of all these cultures are transformed as the result of this process.

Strictly speaking, interculturation is a three-step trajectory. In the first place, what Louis Luzbetak calls individual building-blocks of culture, that is, the signs and symbols, of one culture are assigned functional equivalents in another culture. Here, obviously, translation plays a predominant role.

Then comes the stage of acculturation, in which one culture acquires certain elements of another culture which, in its turn, adopts certain elements and the way of life of the other culture. Often such mutual borrowing still operates at best at the intermediate level. Furthermore, because of the unequal power relations between the American culture and the Vietnamese immigrants' culture, there is the danger that the latter will be dominated and absorbed by the former. Also, in this cultural exchange there are plenty of opportunities for mutual misunderstanding since the codes through which the meaning of the signs of culture are carried may be hidden and different. Often acculturation may lead to either juxtaposition (elements of both cultures are unassimilated and are allowed to operate side by side) or syncretism (the basic identity of both cultures is lost or diluted).

The third stage, inculturation proper, engages the deepest level of the two cultures together, their worldviews, their basic message, as expressed in their philosophies and religions. Obviously, this task requires that immigrants achieve a measure of intellectual sophistication and institutional autonomy that would enable them to confront American culture as equals in a truly multiethnic and pluralistic society.

What has been said about the encounter between American culture and Vietnamese culture applies as well to the encounter between the American Catholic Church and Vietnamese-American Catholics. A similar three-stage process of interculturation takes place. There is the first and essential phase of translating significant English religious texts into Vietnamese and vice versa, a work still to be done for and by Vietnamese-American Catholics. Whereas many classics of Asian philosophy are available in English, very few Christian classics have been translated into Vietnamese. I am thinking not only of the Bible but also of patristic and medieval classics as well as works on spirituality and catechesis. As a result, many Vietnamese-American Catholics are deprived of the theological and spiritual heritage of Western Christianity, and therefore do not possess the necessary resources to enter into a fruitful dialogue with the Western Church.

The next phase is finding the ways by which both the American Church and Vietnamese-American Catholic communities can critique and enrich each other. For example, from the perspective of the American Church, Vietnamese-American Catholics will be challenged to correct their predominantly clerical and authoritarian model of ecclesiology with other models in which the role of the laity is duly recognized and their active participation is fostered, dialogue with the followers of other religions is undertaken, and social justice is seriously pursued. On the other hand, through the experiences of Vietnamese Catholics, the American Church may rediscover the importance of priestly and religious vocations, popular devotions, pious associations, martyrdom, and solidarity with the poor and the oppressed. No less important, in the religiously plural world of the United States, the manifold non-Christian heritage of Vietnamese-American Catholics will be a springboard for the Church to learn from the spiritual riches of other religions.

The mention of non-Christian religions brings us to the third and deepest level of interculturation, which is also the most difficult and challenging. Connected with this level of inculturation are some of the most controversial themes in contemporary theology such as religious pluralism, the salvific values of non-Christian religions, the uniqueness of Christ, the necessity of the Church, praxis for liberation, and interfaith dialogue. This is, of course, not the place to broach these theological issues, but there is no doubt that the presence of Vietnamese-American Catholics will bring them to the fore. Furthermore, Vietnamese-American Catholics are in a privileged position to help their fellow Catholics deal with these thorny issues, since they have at their disposal, and hence are duty-bound to take advantage of, opportunities for theological education that have been denied to their fellow Catholics in Vietnam for more than fifty years.

Vietnamese Americans and Vietnamese-American Catholics: we are at an interesting, even historic, encounter between two cultures and two Churches. The interstice in which we stand allows us neither merely to copy the host culture and Church and thereby lose our identity, nor merely to retrieve our indigenous history and native characteristics, and thereby miss the opportunities to enrich ourselves with the ideas and values of America and the American Catholic

Church. Rather, our betwixt-and-between situation makes us into "the people in the middle," though not "the people of the center," that is, a people who can harmonize the two cultures and the two churches, not by the use of power but by following Christ the Immigrant and the Border-Crosser Par Excellence. It is from there that we can contribute to the shaping of a new society and a new Church. This, of course, is a never-ending challenge and task.

Chapter 8

HOW CAN I LEARN MORE ABOUT VIETNAMESE CATHOLICS?

CULTURAL AND RELIGIOUS RESOURCES

This chapter mentions only the most useful English-language resources about Vietnamese Americans and Vietnamese-American Catholics, their culture, and their history. There is a huge number of works on the Vietnam War and on the historical, military, political, and economic aspects of Vietnam, while little has been written in English about Vietnamese culture and Vietnamese religions, in particular, Vietnamese Catholicism. Also, little study has been done on Vietnamese Americans and Vietnamese-American Catholics.

Vietnamese History, Culture, and Religions

Bradley, Mark P. *Imagining Vietnam & America: The Making of Postcolonial Vietnam, 1919–1950.* Chapel Hill: University of North Carolina Press, 2000.

Buttinger, Joseph. *The Smaller Dragon: A Political History of Vietnam.* New York: Frederick A. Praeger, 1958.

Ho Tai, Hue Tam. *Radicalism and the Origins of the Vietnamese Revolution.* Cambridge, MA: Harvard University Press, 1992.

Jamieson, Neil L. *Understanding Vietnam*. Berkeley: University of California Press, 1993.

Marr, David. *Vietnamese Tradition on Trial 1920–1945*. Berkeley: University of California Press, 1981.

Minh Chi, Ha Van Tan, and Nguyen Tai Thu. *Buddhism in Vietnam: From Its Origins to the 19th Century*. Hanoi, North Vietnam: The Gioi, 1993.

Nguyen, Cuong. *Zen in Medieval Vietnam: A Study and Translation of the* Thien Uyen Tap Anh. Honolulu: University of Hawai'i Press, 1997.

Taylor, Keith W. *The Birth of Vietnam*. Berkeley: University of California Press, 1983.

Tucker, Spencer C., ed. *The Encyclopedia of the Vietnam War: A Political, Social, & Military History*. Oxford and New York: Oxford University Press, 2000.

Vietnamese Catholicism

Phan, Huon Phat. *History of the Catholic Church in Viet Nam*. Tome I (1533–1960). Long Beach, CA: Cuu The Tung Thu, 2000.

Phan, Peter C. "The Christ of Asia: An Essay on Jesus as the Eldest Son and Ancestor." *Studia Missionalia* 45 (1996): 25–55.

Phan, Peter, C. "Jesus as the Eldest Brother and Ancestor? A Vietnamese Portrait." *The Living Light* 33/1 (1996): 35–44.

Phan, Peter C. "Jesus the Christ with an Asian Face." *Theological Studies* 57 (1996): 399–430.

Phan, Peter, C. *Mission and Catechesis: Alexandre de Rhodes & Inculturation in Seventeenth-Century Vietnam*. Maryknoll, NY: Orbis, 1998.

Phan, Peter C. "Mary in Vietnamese Piety and Theology: A Contemporary Perspective." *Ephemerides Mariologicae* 51 (2001): 457–72.

Phan, Peter C. "Culture and Liturgy: Ancestor Veneration as a Test Case." *Worship* 76/5 (2002): 407–30.

Phan, Peter C. "Doing Theology in the Context of Cultural and Religious Pluralism: An Asian Perspective." *Louvain Studies* 27 (2002): 39–68.

Phan, Peter C. "Inculturation of the Christian Faith in Asia through Philosophy: A Dialogue with John Paul II's *Fides et Ratio.*" In *Dialogue between Christian Philosophy and Chinese Culture,* ed. Paschal Ting, Marian Gao, and Bernard Li. Washington, DC: The Council for Research in Values and Philosophy, 2002, 291–320.

Phan, Peter C. "Popular Religion and Liturgical Inculturation: Perspectives and Challenges from Asia." In *Proceedings.* North American Academy of Liturgy, ed. Joyce Zimmerman. Notre Dame, IN: North American Academy of Liturgy, 2002, 23–58.

Phan, Peter C., ed. *The Asian Synod: Texts and Commentaries.* Maryknoll, NY: Orbis, 2002.

Phan, Peter C., ed. (with James Kroeger). *The Future of the Asian Churches: The Asian Synod & Ecclesia in Asia.* Manila, Philippines: Claretian, 2002.

Vietnamese Americans and Vietnamese-American Catholics

Asian and Pacific Presence: Harmony in Faith. Washington, DC: U.S. Conference of Catholic Bishops, 2001.

Bankston, Carl L., III. "Vietnamese-American Catholicism: Transplanted and Flourishing." *U.S. Catholic Historian* 18/1 (Winter 2000): 36–53.

Freeman, James. *Changing Identities: Vietnamese Americans 1975–1995.* Boston, MA: Allyn and Bacon, 1995.

Karnow, Stanley, and Nancy Yoshihara. *Asian Americans in Transition.* New York: The Asian Society, 1992.

Palumbo-Liu, David. *Asian/American: Historical Crossings of a Racial Frontier.* Stanford, CA: Stanford University Press, 1999.

Phan, Peter C. "Vietnamese Catholics in the United States: Christian Identity between the Old and the New." *U.S. Catholic Historian* 18/1 (Winter 2000): 19–35.

Phan, Peter C. "The Dragon and the Eagle: Toward a Vietnamese-American Theology." *Theology Digest* 48/3 (Fall 2001): 203–18.

Phan, Peter C., "Reception of Vatican II in Asia: Historical and Theological Analysis." *Gregorianum* 83/2 (2002): 269–85.

Phan, Peter C. *Christianity with an Asian Face: Asian-American Theology in the Making.* Maryknoll, NY: Orbis, 2003.

Phan, Peter C. *In Our Own Tongues. Mission and Inculturation: Perspectives from Asia.* Maryknoll, NY: Orbis, 2003.

Phan, Peter C., *Being Religious Interreligiously: Asian Perspectives on Interfaith Dialogue.* Maryknoll, NY: Orbis, 2004.

Phan, Peter C., ed. (with Jung Young Lee). *Journeys at the Margin: Toward an Autobiographical Theology in Asian-American Perspective.* Collegeville, MN: Liturgical, 1999.

Rumbaut, Ruben. "Vietnamese, Laotian and Cambodian Americans." In *Asian Americans: Contemporary Issues and Trends,* ed. Pyong Gap Min. Thousand Oaks, CA: Sage, 1995.

Rutledge, Paul J. *The Vietnamese Experience in America.* Bloomington and Indianapolis: University of Indiana Press, 1992.

Takaki, Ronald. *Strangers from a Different Shore: A History of Asian Americans.* New York: Penguin, 1989.

Internet Sites

Among Vietnamese-American Catholic websites, the best is www.vietcatholic.net.

There is a plethora of other fine websites on Vietnam and on anything related to it.

About the Author

Peter C. Phan came to the United States as a refugee in 1975. After several months in a refugee camp in Pendelton, California, he and his family moved to Dallas, Texas, where, after a brief stint as a garbage collector, he began his career as a professor of theology at the University of Dallas. In 1988 he joined the Catholic University of America in Washington, D.C., where subsequently he became the chair of the Department of Theology and held the Warren-Blanding Chair of Religion and Culture in the Department of Religion and Religious Education. In 2000 he became president of the Catholic Theological Society of America, the first non-Caucasian to be elected to that post. In 2003 he joined Georgetown University, where he holds the Ignacio Ellacuría chair of Catholic Social Thought. Besides his three earned doctorates, he was awarded an honorary doctorate in theology by the Catholic Theological Union in 2001. He has published extensively in various aspects of theology, and one of his abiding interests is inculturating the Christian faith and worship into the Asian—more specifically, Vietnamese—cultures.